Who Cares?

Who Cares?

How State Funding and Political Activism Change Charity

Nick Seddon

Civitas: Institute for the Study of Civil Society
London
Registered Charity No. 1085494

First Published February 2007

ISBN (10) 1-903386-56-X
ISBN (13) 978-1-903386-56-9

Independence: The Institute for the Study of Civil Society
(Civitas) is a registered educational charity (No. 1085494)
and a company limited by guarantee (No. 04023541). Civitas
is financed from a variety of private sources to avoid over-
reliance on any single or small group of donors.

All publications are independently refereed. All the Institute's
publications seek to further its objective of promoting the
advancement of learning. The views expressed are those of the
authors, not of the Institute.

Typeset by
Civitas

Printed in Great Britain by
Hartington Litho Ltd
Lancing, Sussex BN15 8UF

Contents

Author

After studying English at Cambridge University, Nick Seddon spent three years working as a freelance journalist for the *Spectator*, *Time Out* and *Times Literary Supplement*, among others, before taking up his current post as Research Fellow at Civitas. In this capacity he has written reports on a range of policy areas, from healthcare to history, and appeared on local and national television and radio. Nick has also co-edited a literary anthology, *Figures of Speech*. He lives in London.

Acknowledgements

It is customary for the author to thank at the beginning of a book everyone who has helped in its compilation. In this case it has not been possible to follow this convention because most of the people spoken to did so under the condition of anonymity. Their wariness of putting their heads above the parapet when it comes to discussing the intrusion of the state into the third sector is powerfully suggestive. Nevertheless, I am enormously grateful to those who have spared their time to share their experience and expertise with me, and whose contributions have added so much to this study, whether or not I have been able to cite them by name. I would also like to thank those who participated in the refereeing process and whose comments have been so helpful in revising the text. Needless to say, I bear full responsibility for any errors or omissions that remain.

This publication has been made possible by a grant from the Nigel Vinson Charitable Trust.

Foreword

There are confidential meetings and confidential meetings. If a meeting is held under Chatham House rules, those attending can say that the meeting took place and report on what was said, although nothing can be attributed to a named person. If a meeting is private, then nothing said at it can be reported at all. If a meeting is held under Privy Council rules, then those attending must say, if asked, that they are unable to confirm if the meeting took place or not.

Of all the meetings I have attended, under different levels of confidentiality, there is one that stands out in my mind for the paranoia, on the part of those attending, regarding the reporting of anything that was said. This meeting was concerned with the relationship between the state and the voluntary sector, and representatives of different charities were speaking of problems they had experienced. The point was made, not once but over and over again, that if any of these comments were repeated outside the meeting, charities could lose their state funding and in some cases would close.

I had been invited to the meeting because I had recently written a book called *The Corrosion of Charity* which argued that there were dangers for the voluntary sector if charities got too close to the government. The response to my book from charity representatives had been largely dismissive: there was no cause for concern, the partnership was fruitful and productive, and no one but a hard-line ideologue could deny that charities benefited from state funding because it enabled them to do so much more good work.

It therefore came as something of a surprise to hear people at this meeting recounting horror stories that were worse than anything I had used in the book. I still have reservations about repeating them ten years later, after the dire warnings, but to give a fairly mild and non-identifiable example: one organisation which received funding from a government department had to send an advance copy of its newsletter as a condition of the grant. A message was received in response to one such newsletter that, if it went out, there would be no more funding, as it contained criticism of a government bill before parliament.

It became clear to me that there were two separate discourses going on: one for the benefit of the general public, who must be kept happy in order to retain their donations, and another for meetings of charity professionals. To put it mildly, this suggests an unhealthy state of affairs, and Nick Seddon's experience in compiling this report has confirmed my own fears. The majority of the people he spoke to in the voluntary sector were very free in discussing their concerns about state interference, but would only speak under conditions of anonymity. This presents problems for an educational charity such as Civitas, since reports should be properly referenced. When so many statements have to remain unattributed, it weakens the force of the argument. However, the alternative would have been not to publish at all, which would not have helped the debate.

The intimate relationship between the state and the voluntary sector has now become incestuous. No longer does the government content itself with funding charities as a means of controlling them: it awards charitable status to its own statutory bodies in order to get the best of all worlds—state funding paid for through taxation; donations from the public (remember the Wishing Well Appeal of Great Ormond Street—an NHS hospital?); funding from Lottery boards; plus the kudos that goes with charitable status.

The Charity Commission has very strict rules about what organisations with charitable status may and may not do. They must be constituted for purposes that are wholly charitable and they must not be formed to carry out the wishes and policies of statutory authorities. In chapter 6 Nick Seddon gives a disedifying account of the way in which the Charity Commissioners have tied themselves in verbal knots to allow local authorities to turn their leisure centres into charities, in spite of the fact that such 'charities' just happen to have exactly the same aims as the local authority and carry out their functions in exactly the same way.

From 43 Elizabeth to 9 Blair

So much for the bad news. The really bad news is that it is about to get worse. The Charities Act 2006 has altered the legal definition of charitable purposes in a way that awards substantial powers to the Charity Commissioners, who are political appointees, to decide on what does or does not constitute charity.

The first and most important legal definition of charity is to be found in the famous preamble to an act of parliament passed in 1597, which was slightly refined in 1601 to become the Statute on Charitable Uses. This preamble contained a list of charitable purposes which was regarded as the last word on the subject for hundreds of years,[1] despite the fact that some of them were a bit archaic, like the repair of 'bridges, ports, havens, causeways, churches, seabanks and highways', most of which came to be regarded as public sector responsibilities, and 'the marriage of poor maids', which has long since ceased to be a policy goal at all. In a landmark judgement handed down in the early 1890s Lord Macnaghten attempted to simplify the rather rambling list in a way that made it more relevant to modern times. He classified charitable activities under four headings: the relief of poverty, the advancement of religion, the advancement of education and finally 'trusts for other purposes beneficial to the community, not falling under any of the previous heads'.[2]

In spite of complaints that the world was changing and we needed a new definition of charitable purposes,

Macnaghten's refinement on the 1601 preamble remained the benchmark until the Charities Act 2006. The new Act retains Lord Macnaghten's categories of charitable uses, with some more added to cover the environment and human rights that weren't uppermost in the minds of philanthropists a hundred years ago, but it introduces an important rider. The fact that an activity comes within the list of charitable purposes does not mean, *ipso facto*, that it will automatically qualify for charitable status in law. It must also meet the requirement for 'public benefit'.

But what, exactly, does 'public benefit' mean? It seems obvious that any charitable activity is delivering some benefit, but does this affect 'the public', whoever they are? Hundreds of years of arguing before judges about charitable law should have taught us by now that everything depends on the precise meaning that is attached to particular words, and yet 'public benefit' is not defined in the Charities Act, or anywhere else. In effect, it will be defined by the Charity Commissioners, who are appointed by the government. It is not unreasonable to assume that anything that chimes with the current concerns of those in government—for example social inclusion and multiculturalism—will be more likely to be perceived as a public benefit than, say, ballet or opera. This represents a seismic shift in the powers of the state over the voluntary sector, but Tony Blair's government has never shied away from overturning arrangements that go back hundreds of years; and just as the 1601 Statute on Charitable Uses is known in legal jargon as 43 Elizabeth, as it was passed in the forty-third year of the reign of Elizabeth I, so we should perhaps refer to the Charities Act 2006 as 9 Blair.

The dissolution of the public schools

Of course we all know what is really going on here. The new definition of charitable purposes reflects the seething resentment, felt by hardline egalitarians towards the charitable status of independent schools. Until now education has been a charitable purpose, *tout court*. Now independent schools will have to show that they benefit 'the public' in some way, or they could lose their charitable status.

The institution that has been mentioned over and over again in the discussions has been Eton College, presumably because its associations can so easily be used by demagogues to stir up class envy. However, no one imagines that Eton College is in danger for the foreseeable future. For one thing it is inconceivable that Tony Blair, educated at Fettes ('the Eton of the North') would countenance it. But Tony Blair may not be Prime Minister forever, and he may find that, like the Conservatives and Ofsted, he has set up a mechanism that will be used in future years to carry out purges he would have disapproved of.

When Henry VIII began eyeing up the monasteries, he didn't start by seizing the Charterhouse. Cardinal Wolsey had obtained special permission from the Pope to reform and suppress corrupt religious houses, of which the assets were used to found schools or colleges, or just went straight into the King's treasury. There was not a lot of sympathy for these suppressed convents and monasteries. Some of them were almost empty; in others there was moral laxity and the rule had been abandoned. However, by the time Wolsey fell from favour he had set up a mechanism for raising funds that Henry VIII fully appreciated. When the King declared himself supreme governor of the Church of England, the wealth of the monastic orders was his to spend as he liked, on royal favourites, a navy, or anything else.[3]

Similarly, the Charity Commissioners won't start off by withdrawing charitable status from Eton College. No doubt there are some small, failing independent schools that are doing a bad job, where there may be child protection concerns, that the Commissioners could go after without incurring much risk of a backlash. No one would come to their defence, for fear of drawing attention to themselves. Then the process could be ratcheted up to bring in larger schools.

We must hope that it won't come to this, but the lack of informed debate during the long passage of the 2006 Charities Act through parliament was worrying. The notion of the voluntary sector as something essentially separate from the state and representing the values of civil society seems to be weakening, and issues like independence and government-creep were not addressed by the Act. This is an opportunity missed since, as Nick Seddon argues in this report, the voluntary sector is in serious danger of losing the qualities that make it admirable, and concerns about what is happening are now the common parlance of voluntary sector gatherings. We need to open up the debate so that those who value and support charities, as well as those who work for them, know what is really going on. This book attempts to do just that.

The making of a good society depends not on the State but on the citizens, acting individually or in free association with one another... The happiness or unhappiness of the society in which we live depends upon ourselves as citizens, not on the instrument of political power which we call the State.

William Beveridge, 1948

Introduction

Voluntary and charitable organisations, almost everyone is agreed, lie at the very heart of a vibrant and dynamic civil society. Engaging in what the political theorist Alexis de Tocqueville called 'the habit of association', citizens come together in common causes to deal with the things that bother them—whether the environment, arts, culture, heritage, sport, education, animal welfare, the plight of the poor, the marginalised, the disenfranchised, or a great deal else besides. What's more, we say that the recipients of charity are not the only beneficiaries, for those who are engaged in charitable endeavours are also beneficiaries, gaining satisfaction from what they do and feeling affirmed by their experience of making a difference, however small. It is good for the people who are helped and good for the people who do the helping. And, since it fosters cohesion and a sense of belonging in community, the whole polity, our social democracy, is also the beneficiary. Everyone's a winner.

People of all political hues tend to have at least a vague notion of the voluntary sector being distinct from the state on one hand and the commercial sector on the other; belonging, that is, to civil society, or what the political theorist Friedrich Hayek called the third sector. Writing for the Charities Aid Foundation in 1997, Lord Dahrendorf said that while governments 'in particular have come to rely more and more on the voluntary sector', the 'creative chaos of associations is what a thriving, throbbing civil society is about. It is the very essence of freedom'; indeed, the 'voluntary sector epitomises what freedom is all about.'[1] Discerning the boundaries of political, commercial and voluntary sectors has always been a subject of debate. The lines of demarcation have always been fuzzy. But few would deny that they used to be clearer than they are now.

According to another authority on the subject, F.J. Gladstone, in a book published in the late 1970s, voluntary and charitable activity could be defined essentially in terms of 'independence and autonomy'. Refining this definition in oppositional terms, he went on to add that 'its fundamental antithesis is statutory action, that is, activity carried out under the aegis of local or central government and their associated agencies within the framework of statutory obligations laid down in legislation.'[2] Few would, on the face of it, disagree. The Charity Commission, the body that regulates the charity sector, has asserted that '[c]harities must be independent of government and other funders',[3] and even the Prime Minister's Strategy Unit avers that where charity is concerned the 'sector's independence is vital to its success'.[4] So far, so good; but all is not as simple as it seems.

While the New Labour government, like the Conservative government that preceded it, talks enthusiastically about independence, this is in truth a concept that is assailed even as it is affirmed. In the past few decades, charities have drawn an increasing proportion of their income from local and central government grants and contracts for the delivery of services, and this in turn has led all political parties to factor them into their policy agendas more than ever before. Notwithstanding the fact that in 1988 he called charity 'a sad and seedy competition for public pity',[5] in 2006 Gordon Brown, the heir apparent to the top job in government, announced in his Budget speech that 'we will now set up in the Treasury, an Office for the Voluntary Sector'.[6] The idea of a state department for a sector that is supposed to be independent from the state should niggle somewhat: isn't it virtually oxymoronic?

In order to proceed meaningfully, we have to be aware of what we are defining independence against. For reasons which will become clear, although there is a lively debate

2

about the relationship between the third sector and the private sector, this book sets out to explore the independence of the voluntary and charitable organisations in the context of their relationship with the state sector.

If there is some confusion about what charity is—and that, as we shall see in the course of the book, is to put it mildly—then it's hardly surprising that we should be confronted with a certain amount of bewilderment as to what charitable independence might look like. Indeed, the debate is very much complicated by the fact that different people mean different things when they talk about independence. Dictionary definitions of the word place a stress on being free to act as one pleases, not subject to the authority or control of any person, not dependent or contingent on something else for one's existence, validity, effectiveness, not dependent on another for financial support. But the very definition is now up for grabs, and we will have to ask, for instance, if it is possible to be truly operationally independent when delivering services under contract for a provider—or if, to couch it in familiar terms, he who pays the piper picks the tune. Likewise, if it is possible to be largely dependent on a single source of funding and simultaneously free to criticise the funder— free, that is, to bite the hand that feeds?

Discussions about independence are now frequently attended by legions of caveats and disclaimers, but this was not always so. Even over the past decade, it has been possible to discern changes in the way that people talk about independence. In 1996 Stuart Etherington, the head of the National Council for Voluntary Organisations (NCVO), the body which represents numerous voluntary and charitable organisations in Britain, asserted that '[o]rganisations which are earning 80-90 per cent of their funds from the state have reached a level of dependency which makes them more part of the state than civil society'.[7] Eight years on, Ann

Blackmore, the NCVO's head of policy, chose to adopt a more semantically elastic interpretation. Pointing out that there has always been some exchange between sectors, she wrote that '[i]n many respects independence is a myth... in reality it is a relative concept'.[8]

And yet, if we were to abide by Mr Etherington's 1996 dictum, a number of charities would almost immediately be disqualified. Perhaps, because independence is a myth, we are not supposed to worry, but isn't it slightly odd that Barnardo's now receives 78 per cent, that the Shaftesbury Society gets 93 per cent, Rainer 82 per cent, NCH 88 per cent, Leonard Cheshire 88 per cent, the National Family and Parenting Institute 97 per cent, and the ironically named West Sussex Independent Living Association 99.65 per cent of their income from statutory sources? Overall, calculations for the dimensions of the third sector vary greatly, as we shall see. However, even conservative estimates show that the sector now derives 38 per cent of its funding from statutory sources, compared with 35 per cent from individuals,[9] which means that the state is now the biggest investor in charity. And this doesn't include the government-payrolled charitable giants—the housing associations, hospitals and charitable quangos—which if factored in take the figure closer to 45 per cent and maybe even higher.[10]

Against every flow there is a counterflow, and however much some may try to finesse the issue of independence, there is a growing body of dissenters who are seriously worried about the changing landscape of the sector. The Charity Commission has warned that '[i]ncreased co-operation [with the state] increases charities' reliance upon the state for funding and, in turn, creates a potential risk to charities' independence'.[11] The NCVO, which wobbles in its own uncertainty, perhaps because it receives 38 per cent of its income from the state, has nevertheless expressed concern 'that the voluntary sector may be perceived as little more than an agent of state'.[12] The Carnegie Foundation has voiced dismay 'about the voluntary sector's increasing dependence on statutory funding in the form of payment for service delivery, its consequent diminished independence from government, and a lack of motivating "fire in the belly"'.[13]

To put it even more cynically, the director of one charity illustrated the issue with an anecdote about a senior civil servant who, when asked by a junior minister what was the best way to nobble a charity, replied that it wasn't to starve them of money but to give them more than they could cope with. Perhaps the most precise formulation of the problem is to be found in a recent study by the charity Community Links. There the authors registered their anxiety 'as voluntary agencies grow and change to look more and more like statutory departments whose function they hope to inherit'. This process, which they referred to as 'animal farm syndrome', is making third sector organisations into 'co-conspirators with government in destroying the very attributes of the sector which, we are both agreed, were precisely the reasons for embarking on this expansionary course in the first place'.[14]

So our inquiry revolves around the question of where independence is being threatened, and how, and whether or not the sector is losing its distinctiveness and the organisations within it are becoming less diverse. In the process a throng of other issues gets drawn into the debate—questions of the balance between big and small charities, questions of the political alignment of individual charities and even of whole sub-sectors, and questions of transparency and accountability.

It may well be, to purloin from one Shakespearean protagonist, that when it comes to state intervention in the third sector we are now stepp'd in so far that, should we wade no more, returning were as tedious as go o'er. But that doesn't mean that nothing can be done. The relativism that smudges the concept of independence is also used as an excuse for never making any distinctions about the size and scale of charities, or about those that lobby and campaign politically and those that don't. But if we do not want to do away with the big repositories of statutory funding, the big charities, the big campaigning organisations—for much of what they do is very important—we will have to make sure that in sustaining them we do not do away with the charities that don't take a penny from the state, the many small, expert, local organisations that don't seek to influence public policy or the legislative process, but which play a vital role in creating inclusive communities, and which are increasingly struggling to survive.

Designated charities enjoy special rights and privileges. They benefit from tax advantages, and from the reputational advantages associated with charitable status. The legitimacy of this status is important for members of the public who give their time and money to charitable activities, since it should assure us that an organisation is what it says it is and that its activities are undertaken in good faith. Up until now, the public have not really been accorded their rightful place in the discussion about the changes taking place in the third sector. It is time we were all more informed and involved. After all, charity really should be of the people, for the people.

1

What Is Charity?

In Lewis Carroll's famous story, Humpty Dumpty declares that when he uses a word it means just what he wants it to mean, to which a rather perplexed Alice replies: 'The question is... whether you *can* make words mean so many different things.' For some time now commentators have been observing that defining the voluntary and charitable sector in this country is becoming an increasingly difficult thing to do,[1] and numerous attempts to make sense of its vast array of organisations and activities have led to claims that it is too complex to define. Nobody would deny that charity is a concept with blurred edges, but the risk is that, like Humpty Dumpty, we use this as excuse for expanding the definition to include anything we choose. Instead, like Alice, we should proceed with more caution, willing to count things out as well as to count things in.

Most charities are united by certain family resemblances, and in order to speak meaningfully about charity we will have to make some attempt to assemble a picture of these common features. But first a simple distinction. People frequently refer to the voluntary sector as if it were synonymous with charity, but in fact charities are separately defined in law. The same assumption of synonymy works in the opposite direction, too: people often speak of charity when they are referring to informal voluntary community organisations like village hall committees and small neighbourhood associations—bodies which may not be defined in law as charities at all. Added to which, although much discussion about the voluntary and charitable sector is conducted on the assumption that those involved in its operations are volunteers, this is by no means always the case. A great many workers in the voluntary sector are paid, and some are paid exceedingly well.

The voluntary and charitable sector

For the sake of ease, we normally lump both types of organisation together by referring to the voluntary and charitable sector. This spans multimillion-pound behemoths through to small, local community groups. It includes large household-name charities, community groups, self-help organisations, religious bodies, social enterprises and some mutual organisations. The organisations are generally understood to pursue social aims and do not distribute assets to external shareholders. Within the sector there are 190,000 registered charities in England and Wales—27,000 of which are branches or subsidiaries of other charities—and thousands more which are not registered with the Charity Commission.[2] For example, very small organisations with incomes of £1,000 or less, along with certain classes of charity including churches of particular denominations, do not have to register. These are collectively called 'excepted' charities. Other types of charities, including universities, housing associations and some schools, are not registered on the grounds that they are regulated by other agencies. These are 'exempt' charities.[3] Include all of these and it is estimated that we could be talking about as many as 700,000 organisations in the UK, of widely varying scale, structure and purpose.

All the indications are that there's a wide gap between the general public's perception and the understanding of the experts. We've already noted that voluntary and charitable bodies are frequently conflated, but things get a whole lot murkier when we start looking at specific examples. People generally think of the voluntary and charitable sector in terms of welfare service providers, but what about arts, sport, heritage, and environment? The top ten fundraising charities by the value of their assets includes, for example, the British Library, British Museum, Natural History Museum, Guy's and St Thomas' hospitals, the Victoria and Albert Museum, and the Tate Gallery.[4] That this would probably be a surprise for many is shown by a recent survey, which found that while 97 per cent of people think Oxfam is a charity, only 15 per cent recognise Tate Modern as one.[5] Widen the category to include charities that don't really engage in fundraising, and the top 50 includes a number of bodies that the average punter on the street would be flummoxed to discover are charities: the Richmond Housing Partnership, for example, the Chartered Institute of Personnel and Development, or the Football Foundation.[6] And what does a homeless shelter in Camberwell have in common with a National Trust manor house?

An exploration of this question is one of the key purposes of this book, for as things stand the simple answer is that they are both categorised as being part of the voluntary and charitable sector. The term 'voluntary' has traditionally been a reasonable way to describe charities and other organisations, most of which are overseen by an unpaid board of trustees, and many of which are staffed mainly by unpaid workers. They have generally also been understood as organisations that do not make profit for investors, which has led them to be called not-for-profit.[7] While the space occupied by the sector is not and never has been rigidly fixed, it is normal to regard it as distinct from the state sector and the market sector. This relationship has often been described as a Venn diagram with three interlocking circles.[8] Each sector has its own space with some areas of overlap. Voluntary and charitable organisations may expand into the space occupied by politics or commerce, but they shouldn't primarily do either of these things.

In recent years an increasing number of voluntary and charitable organisations have moved—or been moved—into the crossover zones. This provokes new definitional quandaries. As we shall see, a number of the bodies that now occupy the crossover zone between the state and third sectors would not traditionally have been described as charities at all. Is it the case that definitions should simply expand to accommodate every body that wishes to benefit from the advantages that charitable status confers, or the good will associated with the spirit of voluntarism? Is it the case, to borrow a phrase from Thucydides, that to fit in with the change in events, words too have to change their usual meanings? Taxonomy is significant because names both define, seeking attributes that organisations share, and classify, seeking attributes that set them apart.

Of the many attempts to define the sector, one of the more illuminating has been made by the American Johns Hopkins University. The Comparative Non-Profit Sector Project was set up in 1990 to compare voluntary sectors of 13 countries. To define the sector for the sake of international comparison, the research team came up with a 'structural operational definition', which requires that organisations make a good showing on five criteria.[9]

Yet when they tried to apply this to the UK, the definition turned out to be inadequate, since some of the organisations that were considered part of the sector for international comparative purposes would not feature in most people's understanding of the voluntary sector in the UK. That is, when transferred to the UK, the definition was found to be too broad, since it included areas of activity which were in reality part of the state provision—such as universities, church schools and housing associations—whose bills were paid by government and local authorities. The authors of the UK report, Jeremy Kendall and Martin Knapp, therefore developed what they called the Narrow Voluntary Sector to contrast with the Broad Voluntary Sector of the structural operational definition. The distinction turned out to be significant.[10]

Table 1.1
Johns Hopkins Structural Operational Definition of the Nonprofit Sector

Organised	Having some institutional setting such as a constitution or rules
Private	Separate from government (this criteria is operationalised by considering the governance structure of the organisation rather than source of funding)
Non-profit distributing	Not distributing profits (to external shareholders) and 'primarily' non business
Self-governing	No external form of control
Voluntary	Benefiting from a significant element of voluntarism and being free from compulsion.

Table 1.2
The Narrow and Broad Voluntary Sector

	Narrow Voluntary Sector	Broad Voluntary Sector
Total income	£12.3 billion	£29.5 billion
Number of employees (full-time equivalent)	390,000	946,000

Ten years on, the closest approximation that we have to data for the narrow voluntary sector comes from the National Council of Voluntary Organisations (NCVO), though this is not sufficiently comparable to act as anything other than a vague guide. The NCVO includes organisations registered by the Charity Commission in England and Wales, plus organisational lists maintained in Scotland and Northern Ireland. It excludes housing associations, independent schools, government-controlled charities (such as NHS charities and non-departmental public bodies), and organisations whose primary purpose is the promotion of religion.

On this basis, it has found that the voluntary and charitable sector has an income of £26.3 billion, 38 per cent of which comes from statutory sources, and a paid workforce of at least 608,000. In reporting these figures, the NCVO notes 'the continuing absence of a clear operational definition of the broader voluntary sector and community sector'.[11] The Charity Commission, which includes within its calculations all registered charities, and therefore a wider range of organisations than the NCVO does, valued the sector's income at nearly £35 billion in 2004.[12] But this still does not reflect the full extent of the voluntary and charitable sector.

Charities in law and the public benefit test

The risk of constantly expanding definitions of the voluntary and charitable sector is that they become meaningless. A common criticism of the Johns Hopkins structural operational definition, and particularly of the narrowed version adopted by Kendall and Knapp, is the lack of explicit 'public benefit' criteria.[13] This has become all the more relevant because, following the recommendations of the 1996 Deakin Report, which concluded that the only way to deal with the diversification of the sector was to create a definition that was broad enough to include everything, the new Charities Act 2006 prioritises 'public benefit.' But Kendall and Knapp were well aware of their omission. There is, they argued, 'no universal agreement as to what "public benefit" actually means'.[14] It is certainly a tricky term.

Charities are distinguished in law by fulfilling two criteria. As things stand, to qualify as a charity a body must have exclusively charitable purposes and it must be for the public benefit.[15] Public benefit is not defined in statute law, but has been developed through case law over many years.[16] If an organisation's purposes lie within three of the four 'heads' of charity—the relief of poverty, the advancement of education, the advancement of religion or the fourth, other purposes found by the courts to be charitable by analogy to an existing charitable purpose—then it is presumed to be acting in the public benefit unless a positive reason for doubt is presented.[17] The Charities Act 2006 changes this presumption, meaning that bodies seeking to acquire charitable status will be required to show that they are acting in the public benefit as defined in law, before the request is granted.[18] However, the Act does not itself include a new definition of public benefit, instead relying on existing case law to provide this.[19]

Public benefit has therefore become the primary judge of a body's status in law even though it is not precisely defined. This terminological strategy is one which could have serious consequences for the independence of the sector as a whole. It is not that public benefit is in itself a bad qualification, just that it is not enough. If public benefit is the only serious qualification for charitable status, what is to stop civil service departments acquiring charitable status? This is not as ridiculous as it may seem: in chapter 6 we shall be examining charities where the sole trustee is a statutory body, local authority leisure trusts, which have been transferred to the third sector in the past few years, and housing associations, many of which take the majority of their money from the state. All could argue that they are acting in the public benefit—but is that the same as being a charity? It could be argued that we have no choice but to work with the muddle: the sector is a chaotic bundle of organisations, so put up with it. There is, however, one preliminary way to start tidying up our picture of the sector, and that is to examine how we have got to where we are; which means that we need to take a brief look at how the sector has evolved over time.

2

How Have We Got Here?

This is not the place for a lengthy history, but even a brief overview of the past can help guard against consequential misunderstandings of the present. It has in recent years been argued that the current proximity of government and charity does not represent a radical departure from the past, but the logical extension of historical trends. It has always been shady and confused, the argument goes, charities have always drawn from the state's coffers, so a tad more won't harm anyone. Though people claim that the traditional understanding is of charity and government as discrete entities, we can't be sure that this was ever really the case. So it's idealistic pie in the sky to wish they might be now or at some stage in the future. It's a case of using dreams of a past that never was to compose dreams of a future that never will be.

Such an interpretation relies upon a rather ahistorical mindset. Ann Blackmore has, for example, proposed in an otherwise trenchant paper that 'if we accept that the relationship between the sectors has always been fluid, then attempts to refer back to a past age... become meaningless'.[1] Which, as syllogisms go, is very curious indeed. One is reminded of Henry Ford's slightly more snappy phrase, cited by the Controller in Huxley's famous novel: history, he said, is bunk.

But while it's correct that government has from time to time had a role in the funding of charity, it doesn't follow that this was on a comparable scale to the conditions that obtain now. That we should have now reached a stage where Gordon Brown could declare in his last Budget speech that there would be an Office for the Third Sector is a sign of how far we have come.[2] There may well be advantages to this formalisation—such as a clarification of those charities which lie within the remit of government and those which have no desire to cooperate and would rather remain at arm's length—but it nevertheless represents a big step, one that few in the nineteenth century, for instance, could possibly have envisaged. To see why, we have to start even further back.

The rise of private secular philanthropy

It's a platitude to say that the history of charity is complex— all history is complex—but one thing is reasonably simple and clear: Britain has had a lot of it. It is difficult not to be impressed by the apparatus that developed over the course of the centuries from the Reformation onwards to support the poor and otherwise marginalized in society. As David Owen shows in his authoritative historical survey *English Philanthropy 1660-1960*, a reorientation of perspective occurred at the turn of the twentieth century, but for the preceding three centuries it had been assumed that the provision of assistance to those unable to support themselves was primarily the responsibility of private citizens.[3]

During the Middle Ages the church provided welfare services, but only three of the medieval hospitals—St Bartholomew's, St Thomas' and Bethlehem (Bedlam)—survived the Reformation, and there were no more built in London until the eighteenth century. In the Tudor and Stuart periods, following the collapse of the institutions of the Catholic Church, most importantly the monasteries, the wealthy merchants took on responsibility for care of the sick and poor,[4] and the legal enshrinement of these changing mores marked a watershed.

First came the 1597 Act for the Relief of the Poor— commonly referred to as the Poor Law—which was designed to support those who couldn't be helped in any other way. It was to be brought into play as a measure of last resort, helping to tackle the chronic problem of beggars and vagrants, and it is not insignificant that the church, which was to play no role in the administration of the Poor Law, was effectively sidelined. Next came the statute of charitable trusts, also in 1597, which simply codified what already existed. Trust Law was intended to encourage more and better charitable giving, to foster a climate of private charity. In 1601, the Charitable Uses Act, referred to as the Statute of Elizabeth or the 43 Elizabeth, was enacted to address abuses of trusts established for charitable purposes. The preamble to the Statute set out a list of charitable purposes that were to be covered by its provisions. While the Statute has been repealed, the preamble has retained a place in the determination of charitable purposes. Four hundred years later our charity law is still based on the same fundamental principles, most notably the four heads of charity—the advancement of education, the relief of poverty, advancement of religion and other purposes beneficial to the community—that define charitable activities.[5]

There has been some debate about the extent to which these statutes did or didn't bring about a growth in philanthropic giving,[6] but there is no denying the tangible signs of change. Take education, which was widely regarded as the best engine of social mobility, since by equipping children with a decent education they would be able to take part in the new capitalist economy: foundation schools and grammar schools popped up everywhere—endowments accounted for over a quarter of all charitable giving in the period—many of which are still around today.[7]

After the Restoration of the monarchy in 1660 came the emergence of the joint stock venture. The appearance of joint stock companies in the City of London which worked on the simple principle of pooled resources—rather than looking to a small number of wealthy individuals for capital, companies were formed which took small amounts of capital from large numbers of not-so-wealthy supporters, or shareholders—laid the foundations for associated philanthropy. Here the principle was that large numbers of people could pool what might be, in individual cases, very limited resources to achieve what, collectively, might be impressive goals. The Society for the Promotion of Christian Knowledge (SPCK) represented one such joint venture. By binding 'the separate and occasional charity of the benevolent into an organised movement for the education of the poor',[8] there were, five years after its launch, 54 schools in London alone, and by 1729 there were 1,419 schools in England educating 22,503 children.[9]

Healthcare was also invigorated by associated philanthropy. Within less than three decades no fewer than five of the great London teaching hospitals were founded: the Westminster (1720), Guy's (1725), St George's (1733), the London (1740) and the Middlesex (1745). Guy's was the consequence of the munificence of Thomas Guy, a wealthy businessman, but the other four were built on the principle of associated philanthropy, establishing medical charities in the leading position they still enjoy in the public's favour.[10] These London hospitals, together with others which were established in the provinces, laid the foundations for the voluntary hospital movement.

A wide field

It is beyond the scope of this study even to begin seriously to examine the extent of the charitable movements of the nineteenth century. When Mr Casaubon conceded in George Eliot's *Middlemarch* that philanthropy was 'a wide field' he was, perhaps, understating the case. Charity was exceedingly diverse. You name it, there was a charity to deal with it. There were charities for the poor, the sick, the disabled, the unemployed, the badly housed. There were charities for the rehabilitation of prostitutes and drunks, charities for apprentices, charities for shopkeepers, cabbies, soldiers, sailors and variety artistes. 'For the cure of every sorrow… there are patrons, vice-presidents and secretaries', wrote Sir James Stephen in 1849. 'For the diffusion of every blessing… there is a committee.'[11] It has been calculated that a large majority of British adults belonged to an average of between five or six voluntary organisations: 'the numbers of ordinary people who would have had some contact with some form of organised charity were impressive'.[12]

A survey conducted in the 1890s found that the average middle-class family devoted ten per cent of its income to philanthropic works, a larger share than that for any other item except food,[13] and a totting up of the receipts for London charities alone in the mid-1880s enabled *The Times* to announce that they came to more than the entire income of the governments of several European nations.[14] By this stage it was estimated that half a million women worked as full-time volunteers in charities, assisted by another 20,000 who were paid. Charities, including the voluntary hospitals, employed twice as many people as the Poor Law boards, and even at the beginning of the twentieth century charitable incomes, not including church collections, far exceeded government expenditures on the relief of poverty.[15] Indeed, 'as late as 1911 the gross annual receipts of registered charities exceeded public expenditure on the poor law and this sum excluded the money tied up in mutual aid, as well as in unregistered charities'.[16]

There can be no doubt, of course, that for the Victorians the evangelical impulse was a powerful propellant, and the zeal of the likes of William Wilberforce and John Wesley during the great evangelical revival clearly played its part. 'British philanthropy, like Victorian society as a whole,' said Owen, 'became tinctured with the evangelical spirit.'[17] It is perhaps no surprise, then, that three-quarters of the charities established during the second half of the nineteenth-century were evangelical.[18]

However, without state money flushing into voluntary and charitable organisations, only those that could demonstrate their effectiveness could survive. While a number of those driving the movement were wealthy—entrepreneurs such as Joseph Rowntree, for instance, along with Titus Salt, George Palmer, Jeremiah Colman, Andrew Carnegie, George Cadbury, Jessie Boot and William Lever[19]—it's worth noting that there were those such as John Pounds, the founder of the Ragged Schools, who possessed only modest means.[20] Although they weren't high profile, the funding for most operations came, not in a small number of large donations, but in a large number of small donations. As Kathleen Heasman has shown, operating in a competitive environment for funds stimulated charitable endeavour:

> As in the business world, free competition tended to sort out the good from the bad, those organisations which showed reasonable results in relation to the amount subscribed being likely to gain further support, and those performing relatively little tending to disappear.[21]

It was the need to be always trying out new approaches, to see which would work most effectively, which gave these private charities their greatest advantages. They were able to initiate new approaches which could be quickly abandoned if they were unsuccessful, or expanded to meet a growing need.

It was in this context that theories of voluntary and charitable action started to be codified. Voluntary and charitable organisations were envisioned as an integral part of a vibrant civil society and therefore of a thriving nation. The political maturity of a country, Alexis de Tocqueville maintained, was gauged by a polity that provided the conditions of liberty conducive to civil society and by what citizens would willingly do for themselves and for each other.[22] For him, state intervention was capable of diminishing the independence of individuals, who, 'losing the notion of combining together, require its assistance'.[23] John Stuart Mill was of the same mind. Without the habit of spontaneous voluntary action, he believed, citizens 'have their faculties only half developed'.[24] In charitable endeavour, on the contrary, citizens affirmed their membership in society by participating in a corporate purpose: in 1912 E.J. Urwick, of the Charity Organisation Society, advocated a society in which true citizenship meant that 'we must feel the claims of fellow citizens'.[25] For people subscribing to such a view, 'charity could not easily be harnessed to statutory provision'.[26]

Such was the prevalence of these ideas that Victorian governments simply sought 'to provide a framework of rules and guidelines designed to enable society very largely to run itself'.[27] This did not amount to rank individualism: 'the corporate life of society was seen as expressed through voluntary associations and the local community, rather than through the persona of the state'.[28] Voluntary organisations may best be conceptualised as part of a range of 'buffer institutions' that developed between the central state and the citizen,[29] distinct from the state yet integral to the fabric of the nation. During this period, the poor law was controlled by locally elected boards of guardians from 1834, and education by locally elected school boards from 1870, which made it easier for a measure of welfare pluralism to exist. As the role of central government in social provision grew, so the balance between the voluntary and the statutory sector shifted.

Reversing the roles

Towards the end of the nineteenth century many people, including some of the more prominent philanthropists, came to believe that in essential areas like housing, unemployment and support for the elderly, charity could not deal with the explosion of demand in a leading industrial society. Not only was the feeling widespread that charity couldn't cope: equally widespread was the feeling that it shouldn't have to cope. Indeed, the very existence of charitable activity was conceived as an affront to a civilised society. Change was not dramatic or conclusive, but if it was gradual it also proved to be inexorable. After the death of Thomas Barnardo in 1905, one critic argued that Barnardo's work in saving so many thousands of children could be substantially improved upon:

> Consider what amount of labour and money is spent upon public philanthropic schemes... consider too if all these efforts were organised and economised into one whole national system for the prevention of destitution and degradation how great would be the result.[30]

Some advocates of state welfare regarded the only useful purpose of philanthropy as 'to force society to do its duty',[31] while in 1915 Canon Scott Holland paid housing reformer Octavia Hill, a fierce opponent of state action, the backhanded compliment of having ushered in the welfare state:

> The voluntary effort that first discovered, by grave experiment, the true nature of the remedy, has, then, by virtue of its very success, to see its work passed over to the official system which alone is wide enough to cover the ground.[32]

To a limited extent there had been co-operation between the state and voluntary agencies dating back to the eighteenth century, although the two had not, in the early years, been happy bedfellows. Between 1756 and 1760, Thomas Coram's Foundling Hospital had received funding from the government, as did the Royal National Lifeboat Institution between 1854 and 1869. Neither organisation wished to repeat the venture, and RNLI is to this day one of the few big charities which does not derive any income from statutory sources.[33] Similarly, although there had been a relationship between the government and certain sections of the voluntary schools movement dating back to 1833, the statutory grants never amounted to a majority of the schools' income, which was still mainly derived from parental contributions. The total subsidy was initially set at £25,000 per annum, compared with a voluntary expenditure on schools of £3 million per annum.[34] Many schools refused to accept grant aid at all as it entailed submitting to government inspection.[35]

The beginnings of contract culture—the arrangement whereby the state pays fees to voluntary bodies to carry out duties which it would otherwise have to perform directly—can be traced to the reformatory and industrial schools. Reformatory schools, as the name suggests, aimed at character reformation. Industrial schools were 'founded to give education, food, lodging and training in the habits of work to a certain class of poor children, namely those in danger of becoming criminals but who had not yet served a prison sentence'.[36] From the middle of the eighteenth century, both types of school had been voluntarily founded and managed institutions; but during the 1850s and 1860s legislation aligned the voluntary principle with state intervention, and both were incorporated into the criminal justice system.[37] Reformatory schools, for example, acquired a punishment aspect: criminals under 16 could be sentenced to 14 days imprisonment followed by two to five years in a reformatory.[38] Magistrates were enabled to sentence children to certified schools, the cost of whose maintenance was to be defrayed by the Treasury;[39] and through grants and inspections, both reformatories and industrial schools were brought under the overall control of the Home Office. It is perhaps indicative of the schools' mixed and shifting functions that seven separate Acts about them were passed in 23 years.[40]

There was always opposition to these changes. A leader in *The Times* of January 1873, for example, complained that 'the practice of relieving parents of responsibility by removing all vagrant children into Industrial Schools would end in casting upon the State the duty of supporting and launching in the world all the children of the poor'.[41] Yet these interventions were, in absolute as well as relative terms, pretty limited—perhaps because of the widespread suspicion of government at the time. Octavia Hill, the great housing reformer and co-founder of the National Trust, wrote in 1874 that 'the principle of modern life in free countries [is] that we are not directed from above, as a tool, but have to think out what is best to do, each in his own office.'[42]

The 1870 Education Act was probably the first serious challenge to the belief that charity and voluntary work could settle social problems. This Act, which can be seen as an extension of the shift already witnessed in the reformatory and industrial schools, committed the state to delivering elementary education where no satisfactory charitable provision already existed. Although the 1870 Act had not been intended to impact on existing schools, but rather to fill in the gaps in the voluntary network, as things transpired the state fast became more heavily involved than had been expected. Lord Shaftesbury, who was President of the Ragged Schools Union, said that the ragged schools went down 'like ninepins' following the Act.[43] The reality was that when the public realised that the government accepted the ultimate responsibility for education, voluntary provision started to look redundant, so the donations dried up.

This perception was encouraged by the competitive power of the state. Many charity schools had to call it a day because the board schools, run by local authorities and profiting from state subsidies, were able to undercut the market. Most of the charity schools made a small charge to parents, and initially the board schools did too, but if the charity school was charging 6*d* a week and the board school was charging 3*d*, who was going to enrol their children with a charitable provider? Then, when the board schools abolished charges altogether in 1891, the church schools were left to compete with a service that was being delivered by the state for 'free'.[44]

The next major development came in the form of the state pension, which was heavily campaigned for by, among others, the great entrepreneurial philanthropists Cadbury, Rowntree and Lever.[45] In 1891 Joseph Chamberlain became the first prominent politician to take it up, and in 1908 the state pension was introduced to provide an income of five shillings a week to all over 70 years of age whose income was below a given amount. In 1908, B. Kirkman Gray declared that 'the problem of the aged has been nationalised'.[46]

For critics of the welfare state, this was where it all started to go wrong; for its champions, this is where it all started to go right. However it is perceived, from this point onwards the state would venture further and further into what had been the preserve of mutual aid and charitable provision. During the five-year tenure of the Liberal government, from 1906-11, the 1908 Pensions Act was just one of a slew of acts of parliament designed to make state welfare provision compulsory, with the 1911 National Insurance Act included in the line-up. The corollary was a revision of the nature and scope of charitable and voluntary activity. As one observer was to say some years later, 'my conclusion is that the relief of poverty should be the responsibility of the State and not of charity, but that charitable relief will and should continue as long as poverty exists which is not adequately relieved by the state'.[47] The roles were reversing: instead of expecting that welfare services would be provided by charity, with the state filling in the gaps, the prevalent view would increasingly be one of the state providing welfare, with charity filling the gaps.

The post-War welfare state

If we hop across to the years following World War II, we discover a series of legislative measures that established the comprehensive cradle-to-grave welfare state. The 1944 Education Act had already enlarged the role of the state as principal provider of education; now came the National Health Service Act, nationalising the 1,143 voluntary hospitals; the 1946 Family Allowances Act, which subsidised families with more than one child; the 1948 Children Act, which covered the welfare of neglected children; and the 1948 National Assistance Act, which provided income for the unemployed. In that same year, parliament finally abolished the Poor Law.

Many of the architects of the welfare state genuinely believed in the value of the voluntary principle. Lord Beveridge, commonly regarded as the founder of the welfare state, provides us with a good example of one who declared his admiration for, and desire to preserve, voluntarism. In *Voluntary Action*, he called on the state to 'use where it can, without destroying their freedom and spirit, the voluntary agencies for social advance'.[48] He went on to add:

> The making of a good society depends not on the State but on the citizens, acting individually or in free association with one another... The happiness or unhappiness of the society in which we live depends upon ourselves as citizens, not on the instrument of political power which we call the State.[49]

By the standards of this comment, at least, it is a pity that so many charities were soon to find themselves facing an acute identity crisis, one that still obtains, competing as they were against the state in a competition they manifestly could not win. They were providing goods and services, sometimes at a small charge and often with strings attached, which the state was giving away free and unconditionally. They were struggling to supply with relatively restricted voluntary contributions what the state could—thanks to the far more substantial revenues of taxation—deliver with more facility.[50] Added to which, charities found their freedoms being curtailed as they were integrated into a system in which the state determined the level of services to which people were entitled as of right. The very word 'charity' started to acquire the shabby, slightly patronising overtones with which it is still tinged today.[51]

Contract culture

It is widely agreed that the Thatcher years accelerated this trend, and in the last 25 years we have witnessed a marked shift in the relationship between the voluntary and charitable sector and the government.

Despite Margaret Thatcher's many fine speeches on the merits of voluntarism and charity, her administration displayed a taste for more control, not less. Although the prospects for voluntary organisations generally looked better after the election of the first Thatcher government in 1979, not least because of the encouragement in the 1980s of a more mixed economy of welfare arising from the desire to roll back the state, it was firmly located in the context of a voluntary sector relying heavily on paid as well as unpaid workers and a strongly centralising state.[52] The new model involved the decentralisation of production and the centralisation of command. Central government set the parameters, the fiscal conditions, which made the mixed economy of the late twentieth century very different from the mixed economy of the late nineteenth century. As Jane Lewis argued in 1995, '[l]ate twentieth-century voluntary effort is no longer autonomous from that of the public sector'.[53]

During the 1990s the Conservative government sought, rather than to give grant aid to charities, to buy services under contract, a system that seemed to hold out the possibility of surer funding. The idea of separating the purchase from the provision of care also chimed with the government's aim of turning local authority health and social services departments into enablers that purchase more than they provide and so promote a mixed economy of care, which was in turn seen as crucial for achieving user choice and services that are both high-quality and cost-effective. Academics have dubbed this separation of finance from provision 'a quasi-market',[54] and New Labour, which has proved no less keen than the Tories to tout the rediscovered third sector, has been happy to keep it going. But there are significant implications for voluntary organisations, not least in the advent of what Simon Jenkins has called 'parastatal entities'.[55]

While government has held out a larger role for service-providing charities, government is also in a position to dictate what services they provide, and how, since it has become their primary funding source. Central and local government departments have a broad purchasing strategy, being free to establish the level of need and then decide how much of what kind of service is required; charities, on the contrary, are far more limited, since they must offer specific services that the purchaser wishes to buy. Third sector organisations have found themselves having to tailor what they offer to what local and central governments are prepared to buy. In this relationship, the purchasers call the shots. As providers, voluntary and charitable organisations have become instruments of the state.[56] A sector which once exemplified the bottom-up approach to getting things done finds itself locked into a top-down 'partnership', with small agencies, in particular, finding that they are marginal, junior partners.[57]

Of course, the attractions for both sides are clear. The upside for the third sector has been an injection of wads of cash they couldn't possibly have hoped to benefit from otherwise. As charity budgets get bigger and bigger, they have been able to increase their revenues to levels never before known in the sector, and at least in theory their expansion has enabled them to handle more cases and meet needs more adequately. Many charities have grown and expanded in response to the funding opportunities, and others still have been formed to take part in the new market. At the same time, the government has been able to resolve the issue of how it delivers a wide range of welfare services on the cheap. Faced with booming demands, which have to be met within a framework of finite available resources, it has been expedient for politicians to resort increasingly to charities.[58] But because statutory authorities are only interested in what is useful to them, the nagging sense of the instrumentalisation of charity refuses to go away.

Any doubt about the scale of change can be dispelled by comparing the figures, for successive governments have massively increased the funds available to voluntary and charitable bodies in recent years. In the mid-1980s, about ten per cent of overall charitable revenue came from government sources.[59] By 1991, government funding accounted for 27 per cent of the sector's income,[60] and that figure is now at least 38 per cent.[61] If we take only the biggest fundraising charities, we find that almost half of their income is derived from statutory sources.[62] Even without quangos and housing associations—which are excluded from these calculations and draw by far the biggest single injections of statutory money into the sector—these figures are substantial. Jeremy Kendall's latest calculation for the sector's dependency on state funding places the proportion at 45 per cent.[63]

Whatever the precise calculations, the state is now undeniably 'the largest single contributor to philanthropic causes'.[64] Tension between the two sectors, with their different agendas and contrasting democratic forms, is both desirable and invigorating, but as Frank Prochaska has argued there is bound to be a cost to autonomy, personal ministration and civic democracy when charities become enmeshed in government regulation and service delivery.[65]

3

The Golden Rule

With parts of our public services critically dependent upon the voluntary sector, and vice versa, the relationship between the state and the voluntary sector becomes more ordered, more formalised. If the broad objectives of both sectors, or departments and organisations within each sector, are substantially the same, then the Charity Commission says that charities are free to work as they want towards targets that the government theoretically empowers them to achieve; but even still it's difficult to resist the feeling that we're witnessing the 'growing functionalisation of civil society'.[1]

We have to bear in mind that it may not in fact be the fault of government if charities become compromised by the agreements into which they enter—as the ex-director of one prominent children's charity has pointed out, voluntary organisations often willingly relinquish their strategic choice even when they do not need to[2]—but there are technical aspects of the contracting process which can straightjacket and subjugate charities, and which can create chronic instability within the sector as a whole. The golden rule is that whoever has the gold makes the rules.

There is in theory nothing wrong with the limited use of public money for the provision of services, but where does it stop? The danger lies in the temptation substantially to rely on such money. How might this affect the character of a charity—or even its survival? How might this be affecting the sector as a whole? If problems arise, not only for those who choose to enter into contracts, but also for those with an alternative vision who don't, then the alarm bells should start ringing. Anything that makes it harder for charities that wish to operate outside the apparatus of the state cannot be good for civil society.

Diversify to survive

There is a correlation between mixed funding and sustainability: the more mixed an organisation's funding streams, the more durable it will be. If funding from any one source accounts for only a limited proportion of an organisation's income, then loss of that particular funding stream may only result in the loss of a specific service or activity. Conversely, if an organisation depends on a single funder for a substantial majority of its income, then that organisation will be vulnerable since the withdrawal of funding could devastate it. For this reason, both the Charity Commission and the NCVO regard it as best practice to diversify funding streams. Though it is often argued that this may not be so much a question of operational independence on behalf of constituents as of financial safety, in practice the two are often coterminous.

The responsibility to diversify funding sources lies with the charities themselves. While the NCVO and Charity Commission both caution against over-reliance, both are at the same time loath to chastise charities and voluntary organisations which have not diversified their funding streams. Those who receive substantial wads of their cash from the government make frequent recourse to two principal defences:

- 'We haven't yet reached the tipping point.' Some charities refuse to take statutory funding on principle; some don't take it because there's none available for what they do; some can't get it; and some of those that do, set a limit. Within this limit they believe they are independent. Terry Connor, director of the Catholic Children's Society, prides himself that they get no more than 30 per cent.[3]

Clare McKeown, head of institutional donor development at Save the Children, which in 2005 received 43 per cent of its income—£56 million out of £131 million—from the state, says that 'many NGOs [non-governmental organisations] would have worries if the figure went over 50 per cent'. The reason for picking 50 per cent? 'I don't really know, it was a mantra I grew up with. It's a question of majority. For us though, it's not the percentage that's important. What's important is whether a government funder supports work which fits within our objectives.'[4] The question of objective will be addressed in due course; but it all sounds rather arbitrary: what's to stop a charity setting its limit at 90 per cent—or even 100 per cent?

- 'The funds are diversified across different central and local departments and offices.' A frequent defence concerns the notion that by diversifying *statutory* funding sources a charity can ensure that no one funder has overweening power. That is, we should distinguish between a single contract or grant and multiple contracts. The argument runs that an organisation which receives 60 per cent of its funding from a single government contract and the remainder from a dozen different sources may be more vulnerable than an organisation which receives 90 per cent of its funding from the state, but in the form of different contracts with different parts of government.[5] Charities such as Barnardo's claim that by committing their own voluntarily raised funds to the relationship they are able to maintain their flexibility and independence,[6] but when their own voluntarily raised funds are so meagre against the combined leverage of the state's funding, wouldn't it be fair to say that their flexibility and independence must be in some way diminished?

At any rate, despite these caveats, charities are aware that the general public may not see things in the same way. At the very least, receiving substantial funding from one source creates the impression that an organisation will be unable to criticise the actions of its funder for fear of the loss of that funding. If in turn the public perceives the organisation as being part of the funder or an agent of it, then its ability to fundraise from other sources is weakened.[7] This anxiety is implicit in the words of Clare Tickell, chief executive of NCH, which gets at least 88 per cent of its money from the government: 'I say to our fundraisers that proportionately they are providing us with fewer funds than they did historically, but they are now disproportionately important because they are the funds that help us to retain our independence.'[8]

Leonard Cheshire, which also takes 88 per cent of its income from statutory sources, goes one step further. It states that voluntary income is 'essential... if Leonard Cheshire is to remain true to its strategic aim... While fees and grants pay for the basic support packages provided to our service users, they do not pay for the additional elements that bring them real quality of life, *the projects that can truly be termed "charitable".*'[9] Isn't this effectively an admission that nine tenths of the works it does is not truly charitable?

If private donations are good for strategic independence, while statutory contracts are not, in what specific ways do the actual terms of the contracts weaken charities?

Broken promises: the Compact

In 1990 the NCVO deplored any move towards contracting on the basis of price-based competition: 'A critical question in this debate is "who does what best?" The concept of partnership needs to be preserved, even if the award of a particular contract has to be made with due regard to financial proprieties.'[10] But it was inevitable that competition for contracts would become a way to reduce costs, and contracting has frequently concentrated on the purchase of provision rather than on outcomes. With a wide spectrum of charities feeling hard done by, the NCVO recommended in 1998 that the government make a covenant with the voluntary and charitable sector. The Compact, entitled 'Getting It Right Together' and consented to by government and a consortium of voluntary bodies, recognised the diversity of volunteering and sought greater recognition for volunteers.[11] As Nicholas Deakin pointed out, such partnerships should enable charities to stay in the mainstream of policy and to improve their services and facilities.[12] Sadly, however, the vast majority of people that were interviewed for this book, and almost without exception those working in charity rather than writing about it, were of the opinion that the Compact is not worth the paper it is written on.

Full cost recovery

Among other things, the Compact was supposed to safeguard full cost recovery. The full costs of a project are the direct costs of running the project, plus a fair share of the overheads of the organisation running it. Public sector bodies, usually local authorities, receive budgets that cover all aspects of this cost, from backroom support, such as human resources, to the staff costs of those delivering the service, to equipment costs. If research needs to be done, records updated, or new transport bought, then public sector bodies are covered. 'No one expects a local authority library to raid its fund for next year's books to pay for cleaning the building's toilets.'[13] When funded organisations understand and recover the full costs of their projects from their funders, they do not need to waste time and energy chasing elusive core funding. The Compact says that for charities, too, full cost recovery should be the norm, and it provides a framework for partnership between public authorities and charities.

Despite concerted pressure from various quarters, one interviewee said that so far all the talk of full cost recovery was 'utter rubbish'. Nigel Haynes, the director of Fairbridge, a children's charity that receives 65 per cent of its income from statutory authorities, was more jovial, though his point was the same. 'Yes please,' he said with a chuckle, 'but when?'[14] A lot of promising goes on in government, but 55 per cent of voluntary and charitable organisations had not had funding agreed for the 2005/06 financial year in advance; and even though government stipulates the necessity of paying for services delivered, 41 per cent of organisations had not been paid on time and had had to use their own reserves to meet the running costs of providing services.[15]

As Rosie Chapman, executive director of policy and effectiveness at the Charity Commission, remarked in spring 2006: 'we know that many charities struggle to get payment for all the costs they incur, which means they effectively end up subsidising local authorities with charity money'.[16] This is scandalous. It makes it all the worse that the assets held by charities are in decline if, as the 2006 NCVO *Almanac* suggested, they are 'raiding their reserves in order to meet the costs of contracts'.[17] Such a wasteful funding relationship can only deliver less effective services. The Community Links survey found that of those members who have seen a decline in grant funding, 73 per cent said it was making it harder for them to be sustainable.[18] And a survey by New Philanthropy Capital (NPC) and the Association of Chief Executives of Voluntary Organisations (ACEVO) found that 86 per cent of third sector respondents believed current funding regimes were adversely affecting the services they offer.[19]

And it is not just the regulator and the bodies that represent charities that identify this problem. Even the

National Audit Office acknowledges that '[t]here has been little progress on reimbursing the full costs of service delivery'.[20]

Short-termism and instability

A classic complaint when it comes to government contracts is the unequal allocation of risk. There is good risk and there is bad risk. Good risk is the kind of risk epitomised by small independently funded charities with the flexibility to innovate. Bad risk exists in a funding arrangement where the purchaser risks nothing while the provider risks everything. For funders, the potential risk would be that public funds are frittered away irresponsibly, and this is what they seek to guard against. For charities, the risk is that the costs of delivering a service to the terms of the contract exceed the revenues from the contract.[21] That there is an 'asymmetry in the distribution of power'[22] has been confirmed by NPC, which has shown that funding agreements still tend to load a disproportionate amount of risk onto voluntary sector providers.

One of the key mechanisms for this is the use of short-term contracts. Local authorities in particular prefer these because they allow them to withdraw at short notice without incurring any costs. From a children's charity with a small public presence, such as Rainer, to big brand Barnardo's, this chimed with people's experiences.[23] By way of illustration, John Grooms, a charity which provides residential care to disabled people, gets most of its funding from local authorities and health trusts under annual contracts.[24] If John Grooms identifies an unmet need and wants to expand its services by building new care centres it will need to take on a bank loan. But the uncertainty of contract renewal makes it hard for John Grooms to borrow. Were they to take on loans and not have their contracts renewed they would be unable to meet loan repayments. Consequently, they would face financial loss and might have to cut services for disabled people. Greater funding security would put John Grooms in a better position to borrow and invest in new facilities and improved care for disabled people.[25]

The more common experience is, as the National Audit Office recognises, a level of 'uncertainty' which can cut into the quality of the work.'[26] Or, as Graham Leigh of the Directory of Social Change puts it: 'Contracts mean exactly what they say and whether it's health, education... or any of the myriad services charities provide, a year of money is a year of money and this type of uncertainty can be ruinous if you're looking after vulnerable people'.[27]

C-FAR provides a cautionary lesson about how wrong things really can go.[28] C-FAR was established in Devon in 2000 to reform persistent and prolific young adult offenders. Offenders were referred to C-FAR at the end of their custodial sentences and directly from the courts as an alternative to custody. The intensive seven-week residential course was followed by nine months of intensive support in the community. Over the five years C-FAR was in operation, 150 out of the 275 trainees completed the course. The majority are still reformed characters—C-FAR's recidivism rate of less than 50 per cent compared favourably to the national average for the target group of 75 per cent. What's more, C-FAR was highly cost effective, with an annual course costing £24,500 compared to £37,500 for imprisonment. C-FAR received less than nine per cent of its funding from the criminal justice system, and the charity had the reasonable expectation of continued funding with the introduction of the National Offender Management Service (NOMS). However, in March 2005 the Home Office reduced its contribution to C-FAR's running costs by £100,000. This, combined with the unforeseen delay to the introduction of NOMS funding, left C-FAR facing a significant shortfall in its budget. In the end, C-FAR's trustees had no choice but to put the charity into voluntary liquidation.

The fact is that, as Terry Connor, director of the Catholic Children's Society, has pointed out, 'if [a charity] loses contracts they are still left with the infrastructure they have built up to support the contracts'.[29] There are numerous instances of this, even for the big charities like NCH, but it is the small ones that suffer most because they do not have the reserves to move around.[30]

Another story, one of insecure finance, inadequate support and big backers who wash their hands of responsibility at the crucial moment, is that of Talent and Skills 2000 (TS2K).[31] On 21 September 2001, the London-based charity, which had helped 26,000 youngsters develop skills in creative media, the arts and web design over five years, went into voluntary liquidation, leaving hundreds of young people unsupported in the middle of their training schemes. When things were going well, TS2K was highly praised. In 2000 it was visited by the government's then 'e-envoy', Alex Allan, who hailed it as a shining example of how community-based projects could close the 'digital divide'. The charity helped create a website for the Social Exclusion Unit's report on IT, for which it won plaudits from Patricia Hewitt, the small business minister at the time, and the education department quoted TS2K's work in a press release about how new technology could help disadvantaged communities in September 2000. When the proverbial hit the fan, however, the support vanished.

Things first started to look bad when in early 2001 the government confirmed that the Single Regeneration Budget (SRB) would cease to exist. One of TS2K's major programmes had been funded with £2m from the London Development Agency (LDA) through SRB round six. The charity had hoped for funding from round seven—but there was to be no round seven. This was not the charity's only funding stream: it bid for money from the LDA's £4.4m Skills Development Fund, for European Social Fund grants, and it had commercial contracts in the pipeline, but it was over-dependent on the SRB. There were two rounds of redundancies, during which time ministers and officials from the departments of culture, education and environment, as well as the government office for London and the LDA, were approached for support, not just by TS2K, but by partners including the Community Action Network. Soon after 21 September 2001 debts were believed to stand at around £200,000, but the liquidators' report is understood to have assessed debts at more than £1m. TS2K paid £15,000 for consultants to review its operations, but the bank cut its losses and froze the account.

The heartbreaking aspect of this story, like many others, is that the instability created in the sector by charities' growing reliance on unreliable statutory funding most severely impacts on those whom charity is there to help. In the aftermath, nobody wrote to the young participants to explain the situation. When they phoned to ask what had happened, there was no answer, and other organisations in the same building were given no forwarding number. When push came to shove, the individuals who were the charity's *raison d'être* were simply forgotten. This lack of communication and apparent reluctance to take responsibility for the situation appears to typify the whole sorry process. As TS2K struggled to survive when grants either failed to come through or came late, ministers who had lauded the initiative just months before were nowhere to be seen.[32] If the 'partnership' between charity and government turns out to be a sham, it is the poor and the powerless who pay the price.

The decline of EU funding for the third sector in the UK, as funds move east to new accession countries, could also have a significant impact. For 2007-2013, a new EU budget has been agreed for the Structural and Cohesion Funds, the EU's main instruments for supporting social and economic restructuring. These funds are allocated over multi-annual cycles: for the period 2000-2006, a budget of over €19 billion has been available for the UK. In December 2005, the European Council reached an agreement that could result in a potential loss to the UK of just under €10 billion over the next six years. This might result in a funding drop for voluntary and charitable organisations of over £800 million for that period, although this is very difficult to calculate with any accuracy.[33] Certainly such changes could represent a real blow to any charity relying on EU funding as a major source of income, although this re-allocation is not a sudden event and UK agencies have known since 2003 that the situation was going to change in 2007. They should have had time to re-structure accordingly.[34] Other significant income streams are also being rationalised or tapered down (the Single Regeneration Budget, as we have seen, along with Community Empowerment Funds, and the declining share of the Regional Development Agency's single pot) with significant implications for organisations reliant on these funding streams.[35] The NCVO has warned that, if current known trends continue without replacement funding, this could create problems for many projects and activities across the regional voluntary and charitable sector in forthcoming years.[36]

To sum up: voluntary and charitable organisations become less, not more, financially secure as a result of short-term renewable contracts, and small organisations are the most vulnerable. Sadly, while in theory a good three-year contract is preferable to a one-year grant, 'experience shows that third sector organisations are making compromises to secure these contracts against competition from other providers'.[37]

Petrol and postage stamps

Another complaint concerns the bureaucratic requirements of funders. Voluntary and charitable organisations repeatedly say that funding agreements incur significant costs in terms of the process of application and reporting on progress. There are a number of reasons for this: dealing with a large number of funding bodies is expensive and time consuming; there is a lack of consistency and uniformity between funders; the procurement process is lacking in flexibility, particularly in the application of government accounting and EC procurement rules; regulatory regimes are overly stringent; and the stipulations on information and reporting are disproportionate to the size of the contract. As a result, resources are diverted away from frontline service provision, creating increased overall costs for the service, which in turn makes service delivery less efficient.

Trustee after trustee, director after director, confirmed that the strings that come attached to statutory grants leave charities in a tangle. Nigel Haynes, director of Fairbridge, wearily described the complications in the system. Fairbridge operates in 16 geographical areas around Britain. That is, there are 16 teams around the country, one of which runs a sailing project. Each team deals with 150 new young people each year. For each project run by each team there might be a minimum of three schools, one LEA and one pupil referral agency to deal with, which means that in order to get the money for each programme Fairbridge must cover five points of marketing and sales, deploying precious resource away from their core business. Previously, under the system of centralised grants, there was just one authority or department to which the charity could apply in order to obtain funding. Now far more people must be seen in order to achieve the same end,[38] and not all agencies pay up after all the effort.

Likewise, the monitoring process, quite apart from failing to adequately reflect work that is often not easily quantifiable, can be a 'bureaucratic nightmare' and, according to one third sector employee, *'disproportionate to the amount of money you get'*.[39] The National Audit Office has admitted that monitoring 'requirements can quickly become burdensome', and that the 'problem is exacerbated where the same monitoring requirements are applied regardless of the size of the grant or contract', but despite a great deal of rhetoric there is little sign of commitment to change.[40]

Haynes gave another example, this time of the facetiousness of contracting bodies. 'Contract culture prescribes everything,' he said:

> This government is obsessed with evidence-led, outcome-driven work, and they demand statistics on every little detail of our operations, from the ethnicity of our clients to their postcodes, which means that we have to dedicate workers to profiling so that we aren't caught out breaking the terms of the deal. An official administering a large national grant [which gave Fairbridge £50,000 p.a. of its £5 million—that's just one per cent] for the Manchester outlet of our operations, visited to conduct an audit. Pointing to the charity's bus, he asked what percentage of the fuel in the tank they'd paid for. They literally wanted receipts and vouchers to evidence the exact disbursal of funds.[41]

Although it might sound like a *reductio ad absurdum*, this is far from an isolated experience. As Stuart Etherington, director of the NCVO, put it, 'government asks charities to account for how much is spent on postage stamps—which is certainly not how it treats the private sector'.[42] The reality is that charities feel patronised by the statutory agencies that fund them.

From the government's perspective, if not from that of voluntary and charity organisations, the new contractual partnership offers the best of both worlds in a litigation society.[43] Audit and regulation are forms of risk reduction, ways for one body that doesn't entirely trust another body to make it accountable. They provide mechanisms for disciplining the voluntary sector. This empowers the audit agency even as it concomitantly disempowers and perhaps even distorts the voluntary agency.[44] The regulatory and auditory burdens imposed by statutory bodies represent a discreet form of coercion which many find alarming, but the truth is that voluntary and charitable organisations can remain free of them if they choose to: it is not necessarily the state's fault if charities enter into a contract with it. It is doubtful—particularly under a government that seems so obsessed with micromanagement—whether the third sector could ever have it both ways, taking the money and not playing by the rules. We must remember that it is not the third sector that determines the rules of the contract game—whatever it might like to think—but the government.[45]

So to a certain extent reasonably, the justification for greater central and local government interest in the reporting, accounting and performance management procedures of the voluntary and charitable sector is that government has a responsibility to protect public money, public trust and public interest. Concurring with this viewpoint, Joyce Moseley, chief executive of Rainer, a national charity that works with disadvantaged and under-supported young people, has said: 'Frankly, when it comes to transparency, if you're taking statutory funding then you must be answerable to how you spend it.'[46]

We should also be careful when talking about regulation and audit that we don't try to fudge the issue of accountability. Certainly over-regulation can have corrosive effects upon the individualism and responsiveness of a charity, but in any charity it would be perfectly legitimate for a funder to expect that it could account for how it has spent its resources. In a small independently funded charity, the accountability might be through personal relationships rather than accounting for the cost of postage stamps, and some charities feel that the greater pressure to demonstrate effectiveness and accountability comes not from government but from their own members.[47] So while some mechanisms for accountability—particularly those employed by statutory bodies—might be worse than others, we shouldn't presume, as Nicholas Deakin has put it, that independence trumps accountability.[48]

The myth of the level playing field

In this climate the smaller charities fare least well. David Emerson, the director of the Association of Charitable Foundations, has pointed out that the vast majority of charities are small and receive relatively little statutory finance.[49] Often, this is not for want of trying, but big charities can afford the professional staff to negotiate contracts on far better terms than the smaller ones can. According to Nigel Haynes, 'it's not just that the big players are more efficient at fundraising and at negotiating contracts, but also that they can afford infrastructure tools which small players cannot compete with'.[50] What's more, when small charities are desperate for money they often feel they have to turn to the state for funding: either they lose out, or they end up tied into unhappy marriages of the kind that big charities can generally expect to avoid.[51] 'The privilege of large charities,' said Dr Chris Hanvey, director of operations at Barnardo's, 'is that they are free not to chase government money at all costs and yet also big enough to take it without being seriously compromised.'[52]

Darlene Corry, head of policy at the Women's Resource Centre, has put this even more forcefully. She believes that government commissioning is prescriptive—and therefore proscriptive—because contracts are always linked to government priorities. According to Corry, the shift from grants to contracts has led to a climate of competitive bidding, commissioning and procurement, which has left women's groups losing out more and more, mainly because they are too small to negotiate with state agencies or to comply with arduous funding requirements. Bidding wars for large sums of money, she says, particularly disadvantage small and marginalised groups because the stakes are so high.[53] When he was Minister of Communities and Local Government, David Miliband told the annual NCVO conference that 'small organisations live a more perilous existence. We must find a way of supporting organisations whose value to society cannot easily be measured by targets or defined in contracts.'[54]

Sadly, however, despite all the rhetoric to the contrary, there are few signs that the government regards the voluntary and charitable sector as anything other than an instrument of the state. Due to 'its instinctive tendency to control processes rather than contract for specified outcomes',[55] the risk is that the government ends up making charities look more and more like itself. In chapters 4, 5 and 6 we will consider how contracting is contributing to the widening gap between big charities and the rest. For now it is enough to note that a contract culture which disproportionately disadvantages small charities against big ones —big ones indeed that are often already heavily dependent on statutory funding—is an imbalanced one. It's not that we want to be encouraging small charities to take statutory funding; but a system is hardly fair if it is penalising, albeit indirectly, such organisations.

Mission Creep

One great fear is that concentrating on acquiring contracts can distort the organisation because it will, through the contract, hand over control of the services provided to the purchasers. This presents itself, within charities, as a fear of relinquishing democratic control of their organisational form. When charities start to take money from the state they tell themselves that they are doing such good work that it is only right the state should pay for it. They assume they will be able to go on doing the good work, but the simple fact is that he who pays the piper gets to choose the tune. Government departments want results. Charities slowly but surely find that they are following government agendas. The more dependent they are on funding, the less independent they are, and the more they follow government objectives.[56]

Grants were never unconditional, but the profiles of many organisations were mixed in terms of service provision, information and advice activities and campaigning. Grants often supported all these and core administrative work. Under contracts, organisations are only funded for the services specified in the contract. For many voluntary organisations this implies a narrowing of their activities. As voluntary and charitable organisations find themselves tailoring what they offer to what the government is prepared to buy, they become distorted. This process, which raises difficult questions about both identity and function, is known as mission creep. At least in theory, the Charity Commission is clear that this is not acceptable. 'Charities must only undertake activities that are within their objects and powers,' it states. It goes on emphatically: 'This is essential. Charities must not stray from their objects in pursuit of funding.'[57]

Everyone in the sector is aware of the risks, but there are few concrete examples precisely because, as an interviewee for the Community Links study admitted, '[t]here was never a day when the [major public sector funder] said we're going to offer you 40 per cent of your income and change the way you are... It has happened very very gradually.'[58] In a competitive contracting culture, unless organisations set very clearly defined strategies, they become opportunistic, in the sense that they will make a short-term decision to bid for a contract because it appears to be an opportunity to generate revenue. All too easily, such organisations accrue a series of contracts which in a relatively short period can skew the portfolio of activities away from the original intentions of the founders or trustees. The Community Links survey reported:

> There may be reasons for being tempted, for instance to protect organisational and job security—few people would feel they had done a good job, or that their careers would be enhanced, if their organisation had to close for lack of funding. Many third sector organisations operate in survival mode, and this can have a significant influence over strategic decisions. However, interviewees felt that organisations had to be much more aware of the impact of these decisions on values, and be prepared to turn down funding if necessary and face the consequences.[59]

Ten years ago research by the Joseph Rowntree Foundation identified an organisation that had changed the sorts of people for whom it provided services,[60] and Professor Norman Flynn has written about an—anonymous—drug and alcohol charity that 'has now moved into the field of caring for people with long-term mental health problems. In this case, the move was motivated by the offer of contracts, rather than the founding principles of the organisation.'[61] We are forced, in a culture where no one wants to admit to mission creep, and certainly won't go on the record about it, to work with anecdotes and case studies: they do not offer quantitative evidence, but that doesn't render the threat any less real.

The match funding problem

When a body is promised a certain amount of money on the condition that it finds an equivalent amount of money from elsewhere, we call this match funding. It is a funding mechanism particularly favoured by central government, and although the following example is hypothetical it illustrates the problem aptly. The Russell Commission is a charity set up by the government to fund charities. The Treasury provides the core funding. It then solicits private sector funding which, in addition to the core funding, it promises to match. So the Chancellor pledged almost £50m in core funding to support the new charity, with a further £50m held in a match fund which is triggered by private sector donations. In theory the proportion in 2006/07 would be 75 per cent government funded, with a further 25 per cent coming from private donors. In 2006/07 it was supposed to draw £10.0 million in funding from the private sector. But by March 2006, only £3.4 million had been raised, over a year after its launch.

Table 3.1
Russell Commission funding strategy

	05-06	06-07	07-08
Core funding	£3.4m	£20.1m	£27.0m
Private sector support		£10.0m	£40.0m
Match funding		£10.0m	£40.0m

Leaving aside for a moment the issues of a charity that cannot attract sufficient private sector income—which is presumably embarrassing for the government because it makes its own investment a disproportionately large slice of the cake—this helps illustrate the hazard of match funding. When a charity agrees to match funding from the government it takes on the responsibility for a project that, unless it can come up with the private funding, it will have to fund from its own pocket. Of course the Treasury's coffers are so deep that it could continue with its projects irrespective of private sector money. But most charities aren't as well off. If a charity has capacity-built in preparation for a new project—that is, upsized the workforce, bought sophisticated new infrastructure tools, and so on—such a shortfall can be crippling. Charities that have undertaken to deliver a service on such a contract can end up reallocating money held in central reserves or, worse, from other projects. In practice, as the NCVO observes, what this means is that a charity 'is effectively compelled to subsidise the project—and puts undue emphasis on one part of an organisation's mission— at the expense of activities the organisation would otherwise have undertaken'.[62]

The strategic problem

The Family Welfare Association began life in 1869 as the Society for Organising Charitable Relief and Repressing Mendicity. In the following year it adopted the shorter name of the Charity Organisation Society (COS), although the longer title was retained for formal purposes. The intention of its founders was to form a sort of clearing house for the many charities of Victorian London by investigating the circumstances of needy applicants and steering them in the direction of the best charity or charities that would be able to help them. It was not originally intended that the COS would offer relief itself, although it fairly soon began to do so. The 'repressing mendicity' bit referred to its intention to stop applicants going from one charity to another—Alfred Doolitle's 'deserving widow that... got money out of six different charities in one week for the death of the same husband'[63]—and to detecting cases of outright fraud.

The COS was controversial from the start, even amongst other Victorian philanthropists, because of its strongly individualistic approach that preached 'the fierce gospel of self-reliance'.[64] They criticised charities that gave out 'doles' —that is, free gifts of cash or other benefits—in a way that encouraged welfare dependency instead of independence. They insisted that no one could be helped until all of their circumstances were fully understood: their home and family, their employment history, their record as tenants, etc. Although critics like Beatrice Webb accused COS of snooping in order to disqualify every applicant from receiving help, this was far from the truth, as an examination of their extant casebooks has shown.[65] Its approach would become the basis for what social workers call casework, and Robert Pinker has described the foundation of COS as the birth of modern social work.[66]

Members of COS saw the open-handed generosity of the rich as a major contributory factor to poverty, because it encouraged dishonesty and led the poor to believe that they could get by without working and without addressing any of their problems. When the unpredictable gifts were not forthcoming, beggars would be plunged into poverty because they had made no other provisions. For this reason they encouraged people to give their money to COS or other reputable charities, that would take a more provident view.

There was, of course, no welfare state as we know it in the early days of the COS, but they worked closely with the Poor Law guardians to ensure that the right sort of help was given to applicants—whether it be charitable assistance to live independently or, if that were not possible, the workhouse. When the state began to assume the role of welfare provider, COS was always in the forefront of opposition, especially to school meals and pensions under Lloyd George's Liberal administration of 1906-11. The COS saw no need for the state to become involved with welfare services at all, believing that the voluntary sector was better placed to deal with problems without creating dependency. As late as 1932, the COS secretary John Pringle could make slighting references to 'Beveridgism' and maintain that collectivism was 'a phantasm' that would soon disappear as society returned to COS principles.[67]

Following Pringle's death in 1938 the COS softened its approach towards state welfare and welcomed the publication of the Beveridge Report on social insurance in 1942. During the Second World War COS started to receive some of its own income from the state: it was asked to run Citizens' Advice Bureaux, and was given grants from London boroughs to do this. In 1946 COS became the Family Welfare Association, and pursued a more co-operative policy with statutory bodies. In 1965 it was decided that boroughs must be asked to pay for family casework in their areas, with the result that funding from boroughs increased from £1,800 in 1959/60 to £49,695 ten years later—over 40 per cent of its income. Madeline Rooff asked, in her centenary history of the organisation:

> Would dependence for so large a proportion of its income on statutory bodies affect the nature of its free choice as a voluntary society or would the selection of clients be made with a view to the expectations of local authorities and their statutory social workers? The answer remained in the future.[68]

It didn't remain in the future for very long.[69] By the 1980s the Family Welfare Association 'found itself playing a supplementary rather than a complementary role in relation to the statutory services'.[70] Towards the end of the decade, the government clearly dictated the terms on which voluntary associations were to play a greater role in service provision, and the experience of the FWA was largely influenced by the changes occurring across the sector. For some time it had struggled to attract charitable giving and its capacity to attract voluntary contributions failed to keep pace with expenditure, so the charity sought new projects that were fully funded by local authorities. It was successful in being able to set up in four new areas, including Milton Keynes and Northampton, but the London boroughs never provided more than two-thirds of the money needed by the London areas for their social work services, and the funding gap, which had been a problem for some years, continued to grow.

The FWA also expanded on a number of other fronts. The Education Grants Advisory Service, which had previously been spun off as an autonomous entity, returned under the FWA umbrella, and the organisation expanded the non-casework side of its activities as well, taking over the administration of more trusts and almshouses. But the bulk of the expansion was funded by money from the Community Programme, a government deal providing temporary employment for up to one year for the long-term unemployed. This meant that the FWA found itself with several projects relatively unrelated to its main objectives, for example a furniture restoration scheme. When the Community Programme suddenly finished, the FWA, like many other voluntaries, was left with considerable liabilities in terms of capital investments. This debt was in large measure responsible for the financial crisis of the organisation at the end of the decade.

The FWA's policy of expansion and diversification during the 1980s stood in sharp contrast to the tendency of the FWA in previous decades to remain tightly focused and to shed activities additional to its main objects. Expansion seemed to be the order of the day, in terms of both financial inducements and the more general political climate in which the 'entrepreneurial culture' was lauded. 'But administratively the organisation was ill-equipped to handle the expansion or to monitor the financial situation. Directors were added on and patterns of communication and accountability were unclear.'[71] The FWA was particularly vulnerable to the kind of expansion that took place. By the end of the 1980s, it was saddled with an operating deficit discovered to amount to £1,500,000 and a very top-heavy management structure.[72]

This financial crisis prompted hefty restructuring during the 1990s. Half of its projects were closed and a quarter of its staff were made redundant. Administratively, a tier of middle managers was cut and the departments were reorganised. At the same time, paid staff eclipsed the role of volunteers and social workers, whose practices had been casework focused, found themselves adjusting to a model that included costing services and marketing them. Counselling services, for which it proved hard to get full funding, were cast off, and the organisation began to run more services for the mentally ill under contract to health authorities. Local authorities also funded services with this client group, which became one of the organisation's most important areas of activity. The goals of the organisation shifted as local offices sought to provide and market what statutory authorities would buy. One local authority strictly dictated the terms of access for users, taking away from the Association all control over its client group.[73]

This is not where the story ends. In a National Audit Office report, published last year, the FWA is held up as an ideal example of a third sector organisation which provides public services. The FWA, we are told:

> provides a variety of services to support families, including mental health services, residential care, day centres, marriage and family support services. Of its annual turnover of £12.5 million, £11 million comes from contracts and grants from various government sources, including Sure Start, the Children's Fund, Connexions and funding from the local Primary Care Trust. The remaining £1.5 million comes from fund-raising.[74]

That is, the FWA now receives 88 per cent of its income from the state. An organisation whose secretary C.S. Loch declared in 1920 that the 'state-aided voluntary society, to some of us a contradiction in terms, and to some a counsel of despair, is not, we hope, the only alternative to the extinction of voluntaryism',[75] and that in the post-war years presented itself as complementary to but autonomous from state provision, has now come to be all but entirely dependent on the public purse. It is no coincidence that in virtually every aspect its mission, too, has changed beyond all recognition.[76]

The ethical slide

In the United States, what has come to be called the 'secularisation' of faith-based charities has been well documented. Two main aspects have been observed, the one to do with adapting behaviour according to the ethics of government, the other altering operations according to the money that is available. The American body Catholic Charities has been accused of changing its mission on both fronts. After it started accepting government contracts, the charity came to define its mission in secular terms: to 'provide service for people in need' and to 'advocate for justice'. For a Christian organisation to define its mission in essentially secular terms, and to be required by law to separate government-funded activities from activities with religious content, could be said to represent a movement away from core values. 'When a person becomes an employee of Catholic Charities,' one worker is quoted as saying, 'I'm not sure they're doing it because of any spiritual thing, or because of our mission. It's a job.'[77]

'If you can't do it the way you want,' Jacqueline Triston of the Salvation Army has observed disdainfully, 'then you'll take your program and fit it into whatever they'll give you money for.'[78] Catholic Charities has also been accused of adapting its programmes to where the money comes from rather than its client base. The state of Massachusetts subsidises a large proportion of the charitable work undertaken by Catholic Charities there. Beginning in the mid-1990s, the state began to shift its funding priorities from other social services to substance abuse. As state funding shifted so did the programmes offered by Catholic Charities. Other programmes, such as child-care programmes and soup kitchens, have been closed and alcohol and drug treatment programmes opened. By 1995 Catholic Charities Massachusetts was spending 80 per cent of its funds on substance abuse programmes that actually served only a quarter of its clients.[79] Three years ago, according to Michael Tanner, director of health and welfare at the Cato Institute in Washington DC, Catholic Charities Massachusetts was receiving 62 per cent of its funding from the federal, state, and local governments. 'Catholic Charities may indeed be an efficient and effective provider of government services,' he has argued, 'but at some point it becomes neither Catholic nor a charity.'[80]

On this side of the pond, some Christian charities have managed to stay firmly with the founding ethos. One such is the Message Trust, in Manchester, whose director Matt Wilson is unprepared to tinker with the memorandum and articles in order to get government or government-filtered money. As a result the charity gets virtually none. It does not even take Lottery funding 'for ethical reasons'.[81] By way of contrast, the Shaftesbury Society is heavily dependent on the state. The Shaftesbury Society is an overtly religious charity working with congregations in some of the most marginalised communities in the country. It used to be called the Ragged School Union, from whose president, Lord Shaftesbury, it derives its current name. Shaftesbury was unequivocal on the issue of state intervention. He believed that it 'tends to debase a large mass of the people to the condition of the nursery, where the children look to the father and the mother, and do nothing for themselves'.[82] Given this aversion for statutory funding, he would perhaps be surprised to discover the charity he headed and which now bears his name derives 93 per cent of its income from statutory sources.

It has not been an easy ride for the charity. 'Last year we mentioned the shortfall in statutory funding for our education and adult support services', the chairman mentions in the latest annual report. 'Whilst good progress has been made, sadly we have had to withdraw from a small number of services where there was no possibility of securing the necessary statutory funding for the future.'[83] That is tantamount to a confession of dependency. One can only speculate as to whether or not the residential care homes for disabled adults are gradually being replaced by more flexible support services because of the changing trends of state sponsorship. Significantly, perhaps, given the scarcity of funds, the Shaftesbury Society is investing heavily in the kind of infrastructure support so beloved of government contractors. There is talk of 'a cascade system of monthly briefings by our Chief Executive', of 'our in-house magazine', of 'our first staff satisfaction survey', of 'a new Shaftesbury Intranet', and of 'a new consultative forum'.[84] The Shaftesbury Society seems to be moving towards greater bureaucratisation.

Perhaps it's now so out of fashion as to sound antediluvian, but in the 1920s William Hodson Smith, the principal of the Methodist charity National Children's Homes (now NCH), stated that 'people do not and will not give up their service to the State'.[85] At the same juncture in history, Barnardo's was struggling to remain true to the zealously independent Christian spirit of the founder and it worried members of its Council that the organisation was in danger of becoming 'the appendage of a Government Department'.[86] In its 1948 Annual Report it assured supporters that it was 'an absolutely voluntary association, receiving no subsidy from the state'.[87] Which was not strictly true, as it was receiving money from the Home Office for running approved schools, but it did still derive over 90 per cent of its income from voluntary sources. The Nathan Committee, which sat between 1950 and 1952 to consider reforming charity law, asked why Barnardo's was not pursuing state funding more vigorously. The charity replied:

'because our job is caring for children and not arguing finance with local authorities'.[88]

How things change. Both NCH and Barnardo's have long since overcome any initial reservations they may have felt about partnership with the state. In 1996 NCH derived 65 per cent of its income from fees and grants, almost all of which were paid by statutory authorities, and Barnardo's 42 per cent. Ten years on, NCH receives 88 per cent of its income from statutory sources, and Barnardo's gets 78 per cent. Both are now big organisations. What influence, if any, has this had?

In 1943 the principal of NCH wrote: 'the Children's Home is a church in the sense that it seeks to direct the feet of those setting out on life's journey into ways of Christian discipleship'.[89] Until three chief executives ago, the person then called principal had to be a Methodist minister, and until the present chief executive they had to be a member of the Methodist church. Yet the most recent annual report has no reference to Christianity at all, other than as heritage. It may be countered that a charity has to change to reflect the society in which it finds itself, and certainly the world of Thomas Bowman Stephenson, the charity's founder, was a radically different one to the one we live in today. Although no one then could have foreseen a multicultural society, it would be churlish and perhaps uncharitable to expect a charity not to engage with the problems that present themselves now, merely because of the way things were. All the same, it is arguable that the charity has abandoned its religious focus for 'values which will find favour with... those [statutory bodies] who wish to work with it'.[90] Since values lie at the core of the charity's mission, we might venture that it is going off mission.

Likewise, applicants for jobs at Barnardo's were traditionally expected to profess sympathy for its Christian ethos. It does not, apart from in reference to its heritage, operate according to those values now. Now the talk is of embracing change, promoting equality, valuing diversity, respecting the unique worth of the individual, and other such popular mantras. As one academic authority has commented, 'many Christian charities have watered down their religious image in recent decades'.[91] Even in 1978, when the Wolfenden Committee reported on the state of voluntary organisations in Britain, it was observed that charities were increasingly 'secular and materialist in outlook rather than inspired by the desire to rescue or evangelise'.[92] No one, upon reading *Barnardo's Then and Now*, could fail to be impressed by the scale and passion of modern operations—or by how heavily integrated they have become into the state's agendas.[93] Whether that relationship is causal or contributory is virtually impossible to discern, but it is unlikely to be *purely* coincidental. Yet, in response to the question of whether or not there has been a correlation between paymaster and policy, a senior figure at the charity, replied: 'I honestly don't think that these changes have been the result of government funding.'

The one that got away

The danger is that, in an environment where funding is difficult to come by, voluntary and community organis-ations become too focused on chasing the funding, without giving enough consideration as to whether or not the funding is appropriate. It is easy to say, and difficult to do, but if voluntary and charitable organisations want to preserve their integrity and independence, then they need to be prepared to walk away from funding or partnerships that do not help to meet their core purposes. There is no need for them to end up dancing to someone else's tune. Honeypot, a charity that runs rural retreats for deprived city children, and the Rainbow Trust, a charity which provides flexible practical and emotional help to children with life-limiting conditions and their families, are just two among many examples of charities which have chosen not to go after state funding because they feel it would lead them out of their core areas.[94] Even more interesting is a charity that has consciously moved away from state funding.

The Sainsbury Centre for Mental Health (SCMH) is a big research charity that provided critical support to the mental health sector as it moved from large psychiatric hospitals to community-based solutions. It represents a rare case of a charity that has changed its focus precisely in order to avoid operational overlaps with statutory authorities and remain innovative. In April 2006 *Third Sector* magazine reported that the Centre, which was set up in 1985, was preparing to cut off a significant proportion of its £4.5m annual income and shed 38 jobs as it embarked upon a quest to regain the fire in its belly. 'We've had a tradition for 20 years of tackling the mental health problems that are possibly the most difficult to tackle,' said Angela Greatley, the charity's chief executive. 'We've always tried to deal with the needs of those people who receive the poorest services and who sometimes drop out of statutory services.'[95]

With government agencies such as the National Institute for Mental Health and the Care Services Improvement Partnership catching up and taking the implementation of these changes seriously, the charity opted to strike out for new frontiers. Employment and mental health in prisons are the two areas on which Greatley and her team expect to be focusing their efforts for the foreseeable future. Despite the downsizing involved, Greatley is excited to be moving away from government funding. 'There was a danger we would have lost the innovative aspect of our thinking and work because we were heavily engaged in delivery,' she told *Third Sector*. 'But there's now this opportunity to really get the edge back.' This is significant as an exception to the norm—a charity deciding to downsize in order to pursue a clear strategic goal in line with its original principles of keeping the government on its toes and supporting the unsupported. Not surprisingly, Greatley came in for vigorous criticism from those who caricatured her as a traitor.[96]

4

Politicising Charity

Whether through being incorporated into the general apparatus of the state, or through the gradual almost imperceptible effects of mission drift, one of the consequences of the widespread changes overtaking individual charities is an alteration of the fabric of the entire third sector. That said, it is hazardous to state that the government is *systematically* effecting this change—largely because anyone who understands government knows how far from joined-up its thinking is. In the 2006 Budget, for example, the Treasury announced provisions 'to counter abuse of charitable reliefs' that 'will prevent donors extracting value from a charity and make it easier to restrict charitable tax reliefs where a charity has incurred non-charitable expenditure.'[1] The difficulty, as we shall see, is that so much of what the rest of the government is encouraging in the sector—such as political lobbying and leisure trust transference—runs counter to these stipulations. Let us reiterate: any government so at odds with itself can hardly be accused of trying to control the whole third sector.

Nevertheless, many now feel that contract culture has effectively allowed the government to legislate over what is charitable—or influence our interpretation of what is charitable—with a resultant political skewing of the voluntary and charitable sector. One of the great strengths of the sector—and of civil society in general—is the space it provides for people to disagree with one another. People can use their money as they wish to support the things that seem to them important. We can give the principle a Voltairean tinge: I don't like it but you do, and I'll defend to the death your right to blow your cash on it. And of course if you find

61

that the body you've been supporting is no longer doing what you once supported it to do, or has been exposed as fraudulent, or has simply become redundant, then you can withdraw your support and invest it elsewhere.

Statutory funding of charities, however, denies us such control over our money. There is something unsatisfactory about taxpayers' money being used to fund charities that are campaigning for things that we may disagree with: the blurring is the issue. If it's a state department, then it should be acknowledged as such, and funded by the taxpayer in the normal way. But if it's really a quango masquerading as a charity, then it's disingenuous to present it as a part of civil society.

The bias to big charity

Like the last government, this government likes working with big charity, and all the indications are that contractual relationships have come to dominate the nature of the partnership between government and the major fundraising charities. Four-fifths of the top 500 fundraisers earn an income from trading fees and contracts, most of which comes from government and its agencies. (The charities earning the most income from trading fees and contracts were NCH with £171 million and Mencap with £136 million.)[2] That government should prefer big charity to small is not surprising if looked at in terms of bald utility. There may be a financial reason for the exclusion of less than mainstream voluntary organisations.

The smaller the contracts which have to be negotiated and monitored, the higher the transaction costs for purchasers. It is both cheaper to negotiate large contracts and apparently less risky to manage the process of service delivery through contracts with large, established, national bodies. So risk reduction rears its hoary head again.

Purchasers have limited management resources to invest in the contracting process. Work with small local organisations takes more time than signing a few large contracts with large organisations. In any case, dealing with an organisation which has an infrastructure of professionals and advice is more comfortable and less time-consuming than dealing with volunteers in local organisations.[3]

The Women's Resource Centre has expressed strong grievances on this topic. 'The widening gulf between Britain's "supercharities" and the thousands of smaller, locally based organisations is profoundly felt by the women's voluntary and community sector', Vivienne Hayes wrote in a letter to the *Guardian*. 'We have seen small grassroots organisations forced to close due to lack of funding, despite their excellent track record of delivering services to the most marginalised and "hard-to-reach".'[4] Contract-based funding mechanisms are not only exacerbating the growing divide between the haves and the have-nots in the charitable world; they are also stifling innovation in the alleviation of poverty. Local community-based charities possess invaluable expert resources, but another of their great strengths is the motivation to find new ways of addressing new problems as they arise. That strength is also a weakness from the perspective of the civil service with their fingers on the purse strings; doing nothing very daring might not achieve very much at all, but it's much safer. So few risks are taken in support of unorthodox groups or causes. While this may be a blessing for small charities—causing them to turn for funding to non-governmental agencies and private individuals—such structural bias in the sector cannot on principle be a good thing.

Some big charities claim that if push comes to shove they would, despite having to make adjustments, be able to take the hit; if this is the case then some redistribution of the funding resources within the sector might offer a viable course. Certainly, an increasingly vocal group of charity workers and politicians is beginning to express dissatisfaction with the status quo, and call for such a rebalancing. At the time of writing both Labour's David Miliband and the Conservative leader David Cameron are shifting together 'towards a localism that could well favour local charities'.[5]

Symptoms not causes

If one bias is to supercharities, another—not mutually exclusive—is to charities whose agendas accord with the government's own general worldview. Put another way, there is some evidence of the squeezing out of organisations that deal with 'unpopular causes'.[6] Looking to the future, this should bother us. If governments perceive charities as instruments to further their own agendas, rather than primarily as organs of civil society, and if they place value on charitable endeavour according to their own political values, then there may come a time when each change of administration brings about a change of emphasis in funding. If with each change in government certain sections of civil society become bloated with money, only to become financially emaciated when a different government takes control of the fiscal ration box, we could find ourselves witnessing a further level of instability in the sector that we would do well to guard against. Changes in administration are inevitable. It wouldn't say much for their independence if charities' survival was connected to the fortunes of particular political parties or even particular politicians. It would, indeed, be a pity if each fall of government in turn prompted the collapse of whole swathes of the third sector.

David Emerson, director of the Association of Charitable Foundations, has suggested that perhaps this government too often has an inherent sympathy that is angled more towards dealing with symptoms than with causes.[7]

Criminology presents us with a neat literalisation of the issue. A senior academic in Oxford has cast doubt on the Home Office's research into the causes of crime, saying that its methodologies are amateurish. The issue is scientific in essence—a stratum of evidence about the causes of crime or antisocial behaviour is missing[8]—but its implications are wider. 'Tough on crime, tough on the causes of crime' is a good rallying cry, for instance, but it doesn't mean much if the government isn't interested in really finding out what the causes of crime are. Another example is sex education.[9] Charities get hefty funding if they promote a safe sex agenda—that is, having sex with contraception—but abstinence charities get nothing. The former—such as Brook, the Family Planning Association and the Sex Education Forum—are linked from government websites, while the latter—such as Family Education Trust and the Challenge Team—aren't.

The same can be said of drugs rehabilitation charities.[10] The current regime tends to support charities that help people to deal with their addiction (by supplying heroin addicts with methadone, for instance) rather than those which attempt to cure people of their addiction (by locking them up and forcing them to go cold turkey). So a charity like Turning Point, which takes 96 per cent of its income from the government, benefits from the current political climate,[11] while small groups like ADAS in Stockport or the Maxie Richards Foundation in Glasgow, which get virtually nothing, do not.[12] It is arguable that these small groups receive little or no government support because they reject the establishment's preferred harm reduction methods: on the other hand, it's possible that if the Conservative party came into power they would reverse that balance.[13] Even if this is a bit of a caricature, we should seek to avoid a system whereby every five years the likes of a Turning Point gets shrunk and the likes of a Maxie Richards gets supersized, only to find the opposite happening five years later.

If charity is to be effective, if it is to add value to civil society, and if it is to provide sustainable support for the most needy members in our society, it has to be encouraged to remain free of such political vicissitudes. This is the responsibility of the providers, the charities, not the purchasers, local and central authorities and departments.

Biting the hand that feeds

'Charities have a proud history of being at the forefront of social change, and any contract that implicitly or explicitly muzzles charities from speaking out for change is a contract they should walk away from,' Rosie Chapman, the Charity Commission's executive director of policy and effectiveness, stated in the *Guardian* in 2006. She went on: 'The sector's reputation for integrity and credibility is an important tool for change and should be protected at all costs.'[14] There is a growing concern that the third sector is losing its independent voice—its capacity to challenge and criticise.

The government professes that it wants the sector to bite the hand that feeds it, and indeed the Compact supposedly enshrines a commitment to this. Some say that charities will be alright so long as they do business with the right departments. That is to say, certain parts of government are apparently more amenable to criticism than others. According to Save the Children, the Department for International Development is particularly good. 'They seek to talk comprehensively to charities—the big ones anyway, like Save the Children and Oxfam—when they're deciding how to direct their policy. We're not compromised.'[15] Others say that what matters is whether you work with local authorities or central government. One political lobbyist, a consultant to some big charities, said that 'local authorities are more of a threat to independence than central government'. When it comes down to it, most affirm that the department they deal with is one of the better ones, so there's no need to worry.

Another angle is that it's not the contracts but the size of the charity that defines how free it is to speak out. The same political lobbyist claimed that it is small charities that are more vulnerable. 'The bigger the charity, the freer it is to speak out about things' he said. 'Big charities are safer, smaller charities are more nervous.' In actual fact, a number of interviewees have disputed this, arguing that it is the big charities that are the most risk averse. So the big charities, and those paid to represent them, claim that the small ones are muzzled and the small charities claim the big ones are muzzled: the chances are that all organisations in receipt of state funding, whether big or small, whether dealing with local authorities or central departments, are to a greater or lesser degree cautious.

Of course, proof of muzzling proper is hard to come by, but anecdotal evidence does exist. For example, there were allegations from the homelessness sector that civil servants made it clear that they expected organisations in receipt of funding to follow the government policy line, and similar allegations have been made in respect of funding for the Refugee Council.[16] One public sector interviewee for the Community Links report suggested that a 'Law Centre that challenges a local authority might find that its LA [local authority] funding gets cut, and it won't be funded to criticise'.[17] Another way of looking at this is to consider charities that shy away from statutory funding precisely so that they can say what they want.

The charity Mind is a powerful campaigning organisation with 209 affiliated charities that focuses on the interests of people with mental health problems. As NPC notes, because only five per cent of its income comes from statutory sources, its 'independence allows it freely and openly to criticise government'.[18] Likewise, the Medical Foundation for the Care of Victims of Torture keeps its statutory funding low: 11 per cent comes in through grants and contracts, the rest through a dedicated team of fundraisers. Maurice Wren, director of Asylum Aid, has said: 'if we're not articulating the needs of the poor, marginalized and dispossessed then we're part of the problem'.[19] These organisations give the lie to the idea that you have to be taking lots of government money to avoid being isolated: it also shows that charities who seriously value the independence of their voice make the decision not to become reliant on statutory funds.

Another issue is self-censorship, and the Baring Foundation has found evidence that when it comes to criticising either policy or programmes some 'organisations censor themselves, in fear of reprisal'.[20] Research carried out by the NCVO and Ashridge Centre for Business and Society in 2002 supported this view. Although the majority gave the biggest constraint on their ability to influence and campaign as cost—which is to be expected—those surveyed cited contracts with government as the second biggest constraint.[21] As we witness unprecedented levels of liaison between charities and the government—there are representatives on steering groups, policy forums, partnership boards and secondments—the question is: have these partnerships dulled the candour of charitable officials and undermined traditions of radical advocacy?[22]

At the very least, we should be wary of what is happening in the USA, where it has been reported that there have been concerted efforts by the government to fund organisations that support it and withdraw funding from those that do not.[23] This is not without ramifications for the UK. During the autumn of 2003 there were, according to the NCVO, suggestions that the USA branch of the Red Cross attempted to influence the policy positions of the UK Red Cross that were critical of US government policy. And in

2003 Interpal, a charity set up to provide relief and development aid in Palestine, had its assets frozen whilst the Charity Commission undertook an investigation into its activities in response to representations made to the UK government by the USA.[24] We should give serious consideration to where the proper frontiers of government influence should be set.

Paying you to tell us what we think

If it's difficult to find explicit cases where a charity has been muzzled by contracts, largely because there seems to be nothing on record about what they might have said, another line of investigation is to look at the extent to which many charities have come to resemble each other. The homogeneity of the worldview of many prominent charities is becoming increasingly difficult to ignore. So many of them sound the same. Their annual reviews and their brochures are like New Labour manifestos. We might say that they are coalescing around narrowly accepted ways of thinking which suit the state bureaucracies on which they depend for funding.

The incestuous relationship between the funder and the provider in the children's charity sector provides ample evidence of this, particularly where research is concerned. Charities that accord with the government's political bias are commissioned to write 'independent' reports that validate other 'independent' reports commissioned by the government, so that a body of material can be built up to support the government's projected policy direction.

The Children's Rights Alliance for England (CRAE) is a coalition formed to lobby for changes in legislation. In 2006 it published a report, *Youth Matters*, which was commissioned by the Department for Education and Skills (DfES), and carries a foreword by the Minister for Children, Beverley Hughes, which gave feedback on the government's

Green Paper of the same name. The CRAE, which has campaigned for objectives with which the government is sympathetic—such as fighting for the introduction of a Children's Commissioner with whom it shared an address for a while[25]—states that it is not in receipt of government funding. Which is curious, not just because it numbers among its members the likes of Barnardo's or NCH or Scope or Save the Children or Rainer, all of which are heavily government-funded, but because a vast number of its many subscribing members are local authority departments and quangos.[26] Apart from the lack of transparency, this illustrates the difficulty of evaluating how much government money sloshes around in the voluntary and charitable sector. And what about the statutory contract for *Youth Matters*? A quick call resolved this: government contracts, apparently, don't count as government funding.[27]

By way of comparison, the Family Education Trust (FET) opposed the Children's Commissioner. In a 2003 report it stated: 'Quite apart from the question of how a statutory office appointed and funded by the government to serve in an advisory capacity to the government can be truly "independent", there are serious concerns that the appointment of an official empowered to "speak for all children" will further undermine the role of parents who are far better placed and equipped to represent the interests of their children than any impersonal mechanism or bureaucratic machine.'[28] This is not the kind of advice that's welcomed by the current government, and perhaps not surprisingly FET doesn't get asked to contribute to government debates. Who needs to talk to the awkward squad when you've got bodies like the CRAE to rely on?

NCH, which, as we have already noted, is highly reliant upon government funding, has produced a number of studies for or in concert with different statutory bodies, as the briefest glance at their 'Policy and social work research publications' reveals.[29] One, the 'Commission on Families and the Wellbeing of Children', is particularly revealing because of the partner organisation, the National Family and Parenting Institute (NFPI). The NFPI warrants a brief introduction. It was set up by the government. Its Chair is Fiona Millar, partner of Alastair Campbell, and from 1997 to 2003 Adviser to the Prime Minister, and reading its latest Annual Review is like flicking through a who's who of New Labour. Margaret Hodge, for example, makes a few guest appearances, and there's even a photograph of the wife of the Chancellor of the Exchequer, Sarah Brown, who presented an award that she had judged alongside Ed Straw and Fiona Millar—at 11 Downing Street.[30] Not only does it take money from the Russell Commission—like the National Lottery, a filter for government funds—and HM Treasury, but the NFPI also distributes the Parenting Fund for the DfES,[31] and it was largely due to administering this that the NFPI's income rose substantially from £1,284,892 in 2003/04 to £7,419,736 in 2004/05.[32] In total, it relies on statutory sources for at least 97 per cent of its income, and it's a registered charity.

Bearing these facts in mind, then, one could hardly expect a report entitled *Families and the State: An inquiry into the relationship between the state and the family in the upbringing of children* to be impartial. For a start, the reader could be forgiven for thinking it is an official government report, so accomplished is the stylistic ventriloquism—it's full of the usual solecisms about equality and diversity. It sounds almost sycophantic. It talks about 'governance of the family', and calls for greater levels of state intervention in the lives of the nation's children. It's also hot on the anti-smacking agenda:

> While recognising that there are distinctions to be made between different levels and frequency in the use of smacking, overall, the evidence relating to child outcomes from physical punishment is

71

negative. There are significant concerns in relation to child abuse and behavioural outcomes. There is also a human right for a child, like an adult, to be free from inhuman and degrading treatment. Despite these concerns… the defence of reasonable chastisement can still be used by parents in relation to charges of 'common assault'. The Commission regrets this state of affairs.[33]

Although the government hasn't granted all the demands of the Commission, and the CRAE will also have been disappointed by this outcome, it is notable that the government is keen to solicit the advocacy of anti-smacking campaigners rather than, say, anti-anti-smacking campaigners. What with calls for 'powerful advocacy',[34] and the endless talk of implementation strategies and more reviews, more monitoring, more databases, one almost ends up asking why the government doesn't just stop funding such charities and write these things itself. Except that it carries far more weight to have an 'independent charity' saying them instead.

Heading upstream

William Booth, the founder of the Salvation Army, famously said that charities spend too much time pulling bodies out of the water downstream, when in fact they should move upstream to stop people falling in in the first place. Many have subsequently interpreted this as an allusion to the importance of attempting to influence public policy, and the history of voluntary and charitable organisations in Britain is replete with examples of such campaigning. One that we have already noted was the call by the great entrepreneurial philanthropists Cadbury, Rowntree and Lever for the introduction of the state pension (p. 24).

It is well known, at least within the Westminster Village, that New Labour has actively courted lobbying. The government's Strategy Unit report highlighted the benefits to be had from encouraging charities to play such a role, and the Charity Commission has parroted this guidance.[35] The idea is that, because charities are supposed to have strong links with the communities for whom they exist, they are well placed to monitor, evaluate and comment upon policies as they are implemented. Having high levels of public trust and confidence, they are better able to represent these communities to the government.

The difficulty of distinguishing between advocacy, lobbying and campaigning does, however, present us with a problem. At which point does one segue into another? When does advocacy stop being advocacy and start being lobbying? Although, on the face of it, making the distinction should be a simple semantic task, in practice it often feels about as simple as walking blindfold through a quagmire. Even the Strategy Unit admits that 'the law is notoriously unclear as to precisely what activities are and are not allowed'.[36]

- Advocacy we can characterise as speaking on behalf of a group of people. An example of this would be a charity like Asylum Aid which seeks usefully to identify problems arising in the immigration and asylum system where they encounter them on the ground. In 2004 the government made significant cuts to the legal aid allocation for people seeking asylum. Asylum Aid had first hand experience of the problems this created and was able to produce a report arguing for change.[37]

- By campaigning, we mean operations that are designed to arouse public support for a cause. Thanks to the likes of Oxfam, Save the Children and Amnesty International, we are all familiar with excruciating footage of famine victims in Africa, or the plight of people suffering from AIDS. We have, similarly, become attuned to the threat of the sexual exploitation of children through the efforts of Barnardo's and the NSPCC. Many will also harbour concerns for the plight of whales, or peregrine falcons, or dogs, due to the publicity arranged by Greenpeace, the RSPB and the RSPCA.

- Lobbying is seeking to influence government in the exercise of its legislative functions, and it is often taken to imply private meetings and conferences with politicians and policymakers. Just as some charities spend millions on fundraising for particular causes, so they spend a fortune on professional lobbyists whose job it is to help them win ministers over to a cause. Often charities are engaged in multiple strategies at the same time, seeking to influence public opinion on the outside while applying pressure within the corridors of Whitehall and Westminster. When it is politically motivated, or more precisely politically *aligned*, lobbying becomes a particular problem.

The Charity Commission has tried to provide guidance on advocacy, campaigning and lobbying. It states that, because such activities can be important to enable a charity to meet its aims and objectives, influence may sometimes be brought to bear where it may further the charity's core purpose.[38] But the Commission is, in theory at least, unequivocal about the proportion of a charity's work that may be comprised by such activities: charities are forbidden from carrying out campaigning or lobbying of a political nature as a primary purpose. Rather, it must be 'incidental or ancillary'.[39] It follows that 'organisations that are established to pursue political purposes cannot be charities'.[40]

Coalitions and other fronts

We have examined the way that CRAE is heavily subscribed to—read funded—by local authorities and quangos, and we also saw how it was commissioned to write a report for the government which those commissioning doubtless knew would be sympathetic to their aims. As a coalition body established for the purpose of influencing policy, the CRAE would commonly be regarded as a political lobbying organisation, though it also has charitable status. This is where the guidance of the Charity Commission proves confused and the reader can be forgiven for finding it confusing.

On the one hand the Commission declares that coalitions can be granted charitable status to campaign as umbrella organisations on behalf of their members.[41] But it also states that 'an organisation set up for a purpose (or which includes a purpose) of advocating or opposing changes in the law or public policy (in this country or abroad) or supporting a political party *cannot be a charity*'.[42]

Guidestar was launched in Britain last year to help foster charitable giving by providing online reproductions of annual reports and accounts that, according to Les Hems, Director of Research at the Institute of Philanthropy, were until then held in the Charity Commission and tax-office cabinets, largely unlooked at.[43] Guidestar is more easily and comprehensively searchable than the register of charities at the Charity Commission.[44] The briefest scan through Guidestar reveals just how much campaigning bodies have sprung up in recent years. What, for example, are we to make of the boondogglish Empty Homes Agency, which receives 93 per cent of its income from statutory agencies to lobby for things very much in the interest of those statutory agencies (such as new powers of compulsory leasing for local authorities)? [45]

Rights-based campaigning features prominently, and, even more specifically, groups founded largely to advocate on behalf of disabled people crop up again and again. They also share a not unexpected trait: a high level of dependency on taxpayers' money.

A few randomly selected examples should serve to make the case. Out of total incoming resources amounting to just under £70,000, Swindon Council for Disabled People received 95 per cent from statutory sources.[46] According to the accounts held on Guidestar for 2004, the Norfolk Coalition of Disabled People was granted £402,000 from Norfolk County Council, or 96 per cent of their incoming resources.[47] The pithily titled Standing Conference of Voluntary Organisations for People with a Learning Disability in Wales (or SCOVO) receives over 93 per cent of its income from statutory sources.[48] The accounts for Breakthrough UK Limited, which provides 'advocacy... for disabled people', show that it took 95 per cent of its money in contract funding from the government.[49] And lovers of irony will be particularly impressed with the figures for the West Sussex Independent Living Association, which in 2004 received 99.65 per cent of its income from West Sussex County Council.[50] Whatever the reasons for this set up—associations sometimes acts as intermediaries for clients receiving direct payments from local authorities—for a charity declaring its intention is to help disabled people 'pursue an independent life', such total dependency doesn't exactly inspire confidence. It's about as consistent as an anti-smoking group investing in tobacco stocks.

In terms of their funding, it is hard to see how these bodies can be called anything other than quangos. In terms of their activities, they are highly focused on 'advocacy': knowing how treacherous is the word 'advocacy' in this context—it often covers lobbying, or seeking to influence government for political ends—and knowing how militantly political the disabilities lobby has proved to be in recent years, it is hard not to regard these bodies as lobbyists. So we have charities established by the state to provide services under contract,[51] and now we also have charities established by the state to lobby. Quangocratic lobbying organisations dealing in highly contentious political matters: is this really how charitable status should be bestowed or how the taxpayers' money should be spent?

The suspicion is that the government is using an ever-increasing number of ostensibly independent charities to drive forward its own agenda, although it is difficult to disentangle the many twines of funding and personnel movement between charitable quangos and statutory agencies. Fathers Direct illustrates this starkly. It describes itself as 'the national centre for fatherhood, advocating for greater support for the relationship that children have with their fathers',[52] a worthy cause no doubt; the fact that much of what it engages in could rightly be called lobbying is evident from the pride it takes in having policies taken up by government departments. So, for example, it says that in 2004/05 the 'biggest development during the year... was the formal introduction of a policy to support fatherhood by the government, achieved as a result of five years of work by Fathers Direct in partnership with the Department for Education and Skills'.[53] The word 'partnership' does not convey the intimacy of the relationship enjoyed by the organisation and the government.

The first thing to notice is that the chair of Fathers Direct is Julie Mellor, who was previously Chair of the Equal Opportunities Commission, which is a named funder of Fathers Direct. In this free movement of personnel, how are we to discern the line of separation? The second is that this is made even harder by the charity's accounts. Fathers Direct is a registered charity that receives 69 per cent of its grant funding, and possibly 78 per cent of its total funding, from statutory bodies.[54] It refers to research funded by the DfES and carried out by the NFPI, and it has in addition been awarded a £270,000 Big Lottery grant that does not yet appear on the books. (In chapter 6 we will see how the Lottery has been turned into a stealth tax so that the government can further its own policy agendas.) This

Lottery grant is for research that is to be contracted to the Policy Research Bureau (PRB). The PRB has just recently registered as a charity,[55] being in the process of breaking off from the Dartington Hall Trust, which is heavily funded from statutory sources.[56] No one at the PRB was able to provide me with figures for the amount of money received from statutory sources,[57] but I was told that the money comes in contracts for research. Looking down the publications list, the majority of the research is commissioned by the DfES, Home Office or Youth Justice Board.[58] There is also a piece of research paid for by the ubiquitous NFPI, which is as good as a statutory funder.

That government departments are paying quasi-governmental charities to produce research is one thing. It gets even more bizarre when these charities are in turn passing the money onto each other in order more effectively to lobby in a way which, because of their combined association with government, is overwhelmingly politically aligned. The Strategy Unit recognises that 'maintaining levels of trust and confidence depends crucially on preserving the charity "brand"'.[59] This is not possible if bodies are not only lobbying on contentious political issues but dependent on that most political of entities—the government—to do so.

Toppling over

A number of big charities are in danger of overbalancing and becoming more dominantly political than they are strictly supposed to be. Some have increasingly shifted the emphasis of their activity away from the direct beneficiary contact—services—for which they were founded and into the realm of political campaigning and lobbying.

The case of Scope illustrates this tendency. Scope has increasingly raised its lobbying profile, and there is considerable disquiet about how it has cut services for the disabled in favour of this political role. In what looks very much like mission creep, Scope was criticised for spending hundreds of thousands of pounds refurbishing its headquarters and hiring several new senior staff on large salaries whilst making cutbacks in services to disabled people. The charity attempted to justify the cuts by suggesting that many people with cerebral palsy would be better off in mainstream society rather than living segregated lives in dedicated homes. The charity said it was shifting its emphasis away from providing services for disabled people to advocacy on their behalf. How directly beneficial such advocacy is for disabled people is moot, which places in jeopardy the wisdom of investing heavily in it. Towards the end of 2005 another controversial story broke, with reports that Scope had appointed headhunters to find a new executive director of external affairs. This individual, assigned to head up lobbying and campaigning among other things, was to be remunerated at £90,000 per annum—a sum equivalent to the subsidy that the charity was at the same time withdrawing from horse-riding facilities at a school for the disabled in Meldreth Manor, Hertfordshire.[60]

This is far from an isolated instance. Briefly, another was the Children's Society, which in 2001, almost overnight, closed all its projects in Wales—causing Rowan Williams, then Archbishop of Wales, to resign as patron in protest— saying it was to shift towards a greater emphasis on children's rights lobbying.[61]

It is not insignificant that the high level of personnel mobility between the third sector and the state or its quangos, giving many routes inside Westminster and Whitehall for political consultancies and the like, has particularly opened up opportunities for a good deal of lobbying. We have already encountered Fiona Millar and Julie Mellor, and there are many others besides. An interesting further example would be Martin Narey, the director of Barnardo's, who was headhunted for the charity after 23 years as a civil servant, his most recent post being as head of the National Offender Management Service.[62]

The NCVO warns that '[t]he decision to take an insider strategy—to lobby behind closed doors—can create problems for the sector as a whole',[63] and voluntary and charitable organisations—especially the big charities—need to think carefully and responsibly about the implications of adopting insider rather than outsider strategies. Otherwise they risk weakening the position of others in the sector. 'If a charity has a large amount of public funding, there is a tendency to lobby in private and not put ideas into the public domain for others to use, which is detrimental to debate.'[64] Perceptions count for a lot, and even if the independence of an organisation has not been compromised, people might think it has. If third sector organisations come to be regarded as being part of the establishment—which would be a reasonable conclusion in some of the cases considered—then they would lose some of their credibility among those who would otherwise choose to deal with them precisely because they are supposed *not* to be part of the establishment.

Since lobbying and campaigning, and particularly contentious politically aligned lobbying and campaigning, seem to be here to stay, how can we clear up the shadiness that surrounds such activity? One way would be to make a clear distinction between bodies that do these things and bodies that don't. Many charities genuinely believe that lobbying and campaigning are important to further their purposes; and yet if no alterations are made to the status quo then there will be no way of stopping charities from becoming entirely political organisations. Which, as we have already noted, the Charity Commission in theory prohibits.

The inadvisability of lobbying too much on contentious issues is not, despite the emphasis so far, confined to charities that are heavily in receipt of state funding, and it is valuable, in order to clarify the general objection to excessive lobbying in the voluntary and charitable sector, to look at the examples of two charities, one, the NSPCC, which receives very little statutory funding, and the other, the RSPCA, which receives none at all.

NSPCC

The National Society for the Prevention of Cruelty to Children (NSPCC) is one of the most powerful brands in the social care field, and it is generally regarded by the public as being beyond reproach. In 2005/06 the NSPCC raised 85 per cent of its funds—about £98 million—from donations, gifts and legacies from individuals, companies and trusts, so there's no cause for concern about the charity's financial independence.[65] But the way the charity spends money has proved more contentious, provoking fierce antipathy in some quarters. In 2000 it was reported that 46 per cent of the NSPCC's expenditure went on fundraising, publicity, policy development and public education, while it spent only 37 per cent on children's services.[66] In 2003, similar figures were reported and a leader in the *Daily Telegraph* argued that 'the charity spends too much on advertising campaigns and not enough on dealing with abused children'.[67]

The 2006 accounts are presented in a very unhelpful manner, making it difficult to calculate the allocation of funds.[68] Indeed, the NSPCC's website is outstandingly difficult to navigate for anyone who wants to know anything substantive about the charity. Eventually, one finds that 83 pence in every pound apparently goes on services to children, but there is no breakdown to support this assertion. According to the 2006 annual review and report, fundraising accounted for just under a fifth of total expenditure, and no one is likely to dispute that activities like research, campaigning and fundraising are legitimate. But again the impression of opaqueness is regrettable: while it appears that 51 per cent of the charity's expenditure goes on child protection and preventative services and projects, closer inspection reveals that a proportion of this is spent on campaigning, which presumably includes television publicity and adverts for its multi-million pound Full Stop campaign, among other ventures.[69] Suspiciously enough, despite repeated attempts to elicit the exact figures from the finance department and the public enquiries desk, no one was prepared to comment. This is more than merely frustrating; it is disturbing that the NSPCC refused to tell a member of the public how it would spend their money.

Ever since the charity's foundation in 1884 it has engaged in campaigning, though not to the extent that it has in recent years. The involvement in campaigning can raise awareness — hopefully thereby changing attitudes and behaviour — but this is not the same as actually intervening to stop abuse. It would seem that the service aspect has decreased as a proportion of the charity's overall work. In the past it did more frontline investigative and preventative child protection work, and much of the donating public still perceive this to be the case.

The NSPCC has come in for particular criticism over the years for its methods of fundraising and campaigning. For example, last year 450 guests were flown out to a charity ball in St Petersburg where the tickets cost £5,000 each — a party *The Independent* said 'even the tsars might have found a little over-indulgent' — to raise money for the charity.[70] One former employee, criticising the rise of managerialism and decline of frontline services, has complained about how the charity 'has lost its way' since the early nineties because it 'has become more interested in its own perceived status than the service it was set up to provide'.[71] Another said that '[a]lthough the legal powers vested in the NSPCC to protect children have, in theory, never been revoked, the infrastructure necessary to make these of any use in protecting children no longer exists'.[72]

The Charity Commission states that 'charities should ensure that [research] is properly conducted using robust and objective research methods',[73] but in 2003 the charity was accused of running a campaign on false pretences. The campaign in question was a £1 million effort to criminalise smacking.[74] 'The NSPCC declared—adducing as evidence a poll it conducted—that the majority of parents supported legal reform against smacking. But it turned out that the pollsters had asked what people thought about "hitting" children, which has entirely different implications.'[75] The NSPCC has also been arraigned for using rickety research, presented as incontrovertible evidence, in making its case for a ban on smacking. On 4 July 2004 BBC1's *Politics Show* broadcast the following statement:

> On our programme three weeks ago, we carried an item about the possibility of a ban on smacking, and in that film we stated that in Sweden where they have a ban on smacking, only four children have died from child abuse in 25 years, whereas in the UK the equivalent figure is one a week.
>
> Now, we got these figures from the NSPCC and they are, indeed, startling, but alas they are also misleading. In fact, according to the Swedish Bureau of Statistics and Unicef, the rate of child mortality at the hands of parents or carers in Sweden is at a comparable level with the UK, and we are very happy to correct that impression.[76]

The NSPCC's approach to raising public awareness is perhaps epitomised by its most controversial effort, the Full Stop campaign, launched in March 1999 at the same time as 88 members of staff were made redundant.[77] The campaign, for which the appeal total in 2006 stood at £187 million, calls for an end to cruelty to children—which presumably translates to a call for a universal change in human nature. A number of commentators find this unconvincing, if not manipulative, because, they say, of its almost panglossian scope. According to one columnist in the *Guardian*: 'The efficacy of these efforts is questionable. The NSPCC has been around since 1884, but the level of child abuse has remained constant. Yet posters in bus shelters, rather than hands-on help, is the charity's preferred way of tackling child abuse.'[78] Some years ago, a leader in *Community Care* magazine said:

> when the aim… is arguably unrealistic, questions must be asked when millions are poured into activities whose outcomes for children are far less obvious than those of the organisation's children's services. Is the NSPCC carried away with its own importance? It's not hard to see that the aim of protecting children can be furthered more successfully if the NSPCC is strong and well funded. But that should not make the growth and high profile of the NSPCC ends in themselves.[79]

The author of the *Guardian* piece concluded with the extraordinarily strident recommendation that 'this avaricious organisation, inflated by its own sense of self-importance, doesn't need to be restructured: it needs to be dismantled'.[80] Whether or not one agrees with these sentiments, the fact that the NSPCC has provoked such indignation indicates that the charity should reconsider both its campaigning practices and the balance of campaigning and service delivery in its allocation of resources.

RSPCA

The Royal Society for the Prevention of Cruelty to Animals (RSPCA) illustrates how badly things can go wrong when a charity becomes highly politicised. Founded in 1824, the RSPCA has been around for so long and done so much good that it has become a national treasure. It's the first and largest animal charity in the world, and our love of fluffy bunnies and permed poodles—the fact that we are a nation of what Orwell calls pigeon-fanciers—owes much to the charity's work. It has always run a wide range of services for the protection of animals in Britain, and to some extent it still does. However, in recent years the character of the organisation has changed, moving from animal welfare to animal rights and diverting funds from services for animals to lobbying and campaigning.

The composition of the charity's ruling council graphically exhibits this shift. In 2002, Jackie Ballard, a former Liberal Democrat MP with no managerial experience — she had never run a business or a charity in her life — was elected to be director-general of the charity. Her main qualification for being in charge of a workforce of almost two thousand people and a multimillion-pound budget was her vehement opposition to hunting, and the appointment represented something of a victory for the animal rights movement's long campaign to seize control of the RSPCA.[81] It was Richard Ryder, previously head of the Political Animal Lobby, as well as being a former chairman and now a council member, who put her up for the job. Jacq Denham, a council member involved in the selection process who has since resigned in protest at the result, said: 'Mrs Ballard was asked the difference between cash flow forecasts and management accounts and said she had never even heard the terms. It beggars belief that she was offered the job.'[82]

Jackie Ballard was not the only animal rights activist parachuted into a senior post at the charity. In 2004, 50 per cent of candidates for council posts were members of the League Against Cruel Sports and Compassion in World Farming. Five belong to the British Union for the Abolition of Vivisection, and two are members of People for the Ethical Treatment of Animals. All want foxhunting banned.[83]

This political colonisation of the charity is disturbing, not least because some of the charity's new affiliates are bodies that, rather than receiving government money, have actually *given* money to the Labour party in the hope of influencing its attitude towards the animal rights lobby. The RSPCA formed an umbrella group—the Campaign for the Protection of the Hunted Animal—along with the League Against Cruel Sports and the International Fund for Animal Welfare (IFAW), a profit-making company which has pumped millions of pounds into the anti-hunting campaign in this country, and organised a £1 million donation to the Labour party before the 1997 election, under the guise of Richard Ryder's Political Animal Lobby.[84] The League, meanwhile, gave the Labour party £80,000 in 1979, some of which Labour was forced to return.[85]

These policy moves have led to the defections of a number of members despairing of the RSPCA's political strategy.[86] Perhaps the most high profile casualty has been Richard Meade, three-times Olympic gold-medal winner, kicked out for trying to increase countryside membership.[87] These internal skirmishes are significant inasmuch as they have altered the charity's posture as a lobbying body. This in turn raises important questions about what a charity chooses to address—and therefore how it chooses to channel its resources—and the manner in which it chooses to do so. And the RSPCA has become something of a test case for how not to engage in political campaigning.

Firstly, it fails to comply with the Charity Commission's guidance on the use of emotive material. The Charity Commission states that 'charities should ensure that [research] is properly conducted using robust and objective research methods':[88] what's more, 'charities need to consider the particular risks of using emotive materials, which may be significant because such materials can be controversial and potentially adversely affect the public's perception and attitude towards the charity'.[89] This is actually a widespread problem—even the RSPB has had its knuckles rapped a few times by both the Advertising Standards Authority and Parliament in recent years[90]—because everyone is trying to grab attention in an increasingly rivalrous environment.

Right from the off, when a bill first came before Parliament seeking to ban all blood sports including foxhunting, the RSPCA and the IFAW reportedly spent some £3 million in three weeks on shocking advertisements in support of this bill. While the drama of a campaign might bring a satisfying jag of publicity, in the long-term charities' reputations are endangered.

Secondly, and relatedly, like the NSPCC, it has made publicity an end in itself. That this is the case is evident from its annual report. 'According to monthly reports compiled by the trade paper *PR Week*,' the report boasts, 'the RSPCA is consistently one of the top five non-governmental organisations achieving print and online coverage, higher than most other charities. No other animal charity appears in the top 10.'[91] The Charity Commission warns against 'types of campaigning and political activities [that] could—if they are not properly managed—damage the charity's reputation'.[92] Early in 2006, in a case that had been running for two years, the charity unsuccessfully attempted to prosecute PC Jonathan Bell for killing a cat with a spade. On the face of it that perhaps sounds reasonable—except that the cat had been run over, PC Bell had been told the RSPCA couldn't be contacted, and he needed to put the creature out of its misery. From the RSPCA's perspective, the stunt backfired: PC Bell was acquitted and the charity was denied the right to appeal. Chris Newman, of the Federation of Companion Animal Societies, said: 'I think the issue is that the RSPCA has become too much of a political campaigning body and that prosecutions have become an easy way to raise profile and money.'[93] Such a conflict of interest between prosecuting and fundraising roles—using high-profile prosecutions to gain maximum publicity and attract funding—can only undermine public confidence.

Thirdly, it contravenes the Charity Commission's guidance on the role of campaigning. The RSPCA's 'Back off

Badgers' is a campaign against the government's proposals to cull badgers over fears that they spread tuberculosis among cattle. However, it relies on emotive material to make a case with an at best contentious scientific base, and it really becomes an issue of defending the welfare of one animal in favour of another. To recap, political activity is allowed if it is ancillary to the organisation's charitable aims. That is, charities are permitted to engage in political campaigning if it furthers the purposes of the charity and only to the extent that it is justified by the resources applied. Now, admittedly, the Commission's guidelines leave rather too much latitude, and this in itself needs revising; but even despite the ambiguity, it is difficult to see how the 'Back off Badgers' campaign is ancillary to the charity's aims. The charity is allocating resources to political ends that can hardly be said to be part of its remit. Because the campaign is solely political, it is inconsistent with the status and purposes of the RSPCA as a charitable body. The charity has become a pressure group. 'It is perfectly at liberty to engage in political campaigning,' Stanley Brodie QC has pointed out, 'but if it does it should not maintain its tax-free status.'[94]

All of these issues, and others to boot, come together when we examine the RSPCA's conduct with regard to foxhunting. It is worth noting that some of the founding members were Masters of Foxhounds, and that in its evidence to the Scott Henderson Inquiry, which reported in 1951, the RSPCA's position was that hunting was a more humane method of controlling foxes than shooting. If its views have changed, that has less to do with scientific evidence than politics. Llin Golding, a pro-hunting Labour peer, has even suggested that the whole fiasco has been 'all about pay-back time for the miners'[95]—presumably implying a kind of proxy revenge against the upper classes. There are others, too, who believe that the RSPCA's anti-hunting policy is 'led more by a hatred of hunting than willingness to improve animal welfare'.[96]

The source of those words is significant: they aren't those of some nutty tweed-wearing beagler, but John Hobhouse, who, as well as having notched up 50 years of membership, and 25 years on the ruling council, was also for seven years the charity's national chairman. Hobhouse was described by the historian of the Society, Anthony Brown, as 'likely to go down in the Society's history as the first great reforming chairman who set up detailed specialist committees on factory farming, export of live animals, vivisection and homeless animals etc, and introduced top-class scientists, whose advice was welcomed by Government Ministers'.[97] Now in his nineties, Hobhouse has repeatedly expressed his dismay about the way that things have gone.[98]

When mounting campaigns, charities have a responsibility to argue along rational, scientific lines. Unpleasant as the whole business is, some exploration of the foxhunting debate is necessary to show how the RSPCA has fallen short of this requirement—and to show why charities should be wary of lobbying on contentious political matters. The RSPCA, does, of course, protest that it is reasonable. 'The RSPCA's policy on hunting,' according to Jackie Ballard, 'has been developed over many years on the basis of a large body of scientific and technical advice.'[99] But this 'scientific and technical advice' is highly moot. So, for instance, the RSPCA has argued that shooting is better than hunting. Yet when the All Party Parliamentary Middle Way Group (APPMWG) commissioned a report, its conclusions showed that in extensive trials shooting foxes invariably results in an unacceptably high degree of wounding.

In actual fact, the hunting business also compromised the National Trust, as Charlie Pye-Smith has demonstrated in his recent book. A report commissioned by the National Trust in 1996 concluded that hunting caused considerable suffering, and the Trust immediately banned the hunting of red deer on its land. But that report came in for heavy criticism, and the original authors in fact revised their conclusions on a joint review of their findings for the Burns Inquiry in 2000.[100] The revised interpretation of the data undermined the case for banning hunting. 'The implications of this were stark: the National Trust had introduced a hunting ban on the back of dubious scientific evidence.'[101] The whole saga 'shows what happens when decisions are made on the basis of contentious, or disputed, scientific opinion'.[102]

If, as it claims, the RSPCA's lobbying and campaigning is based upon such solid scientific research, it is curious that it has not been forthcoming with it. Frequent questions addressed by the three co-chairs of the APPMWG, Peter Luff, Lembit Öpik and Baroness Golding, have not been answered by the RSPCA, IFAW or the League Against Cruel Sports. 'I am disappointed, but not surprised, by the RSPCA's inability to respond, logically, with facts, to the questions I have asked', Lembit Öpik has said. 'I am not surprised, because the answers to my questions would require them to change their position.'[103]

The fact is that for a charity which presents its objects as being so singular, the RSPCA turns out to be rather mixed-up. Indeed, as has been convincingly demonstrated, the RSPCA's position is not consistent with a concern for the welfare of animals in the wild, for it relies on 'a confused ethical base'.[104] Isn't it odd that the charity should be categorically 'opposed to shooting for sport' and to the 'hunting of animals with dogs or other animals', yet tolerate falconry, sport angling and commercial fishing?[105] Since Britain's nine million domestic cats kill at least 88 million wild birds and around 164 million small mammals every year, exceeding the number of wild animals killed by dogs by a factor of over 12,000, shouldn't something be done about our country's moggies?[106] 'What the RSPCA cannot deny is that it has made an enormous and expensive fuss about hunting, an activity which kills relatively few animals, and has remained silent on other issues of major importance for animal welfare.'[107]

The RSPCA's emotive campaigning and lobbying, which makes nonsense of the legal requirement not to be politically motivated but to keep such activities ancillary to the charity's stated objects, has been criticised repeatedly in recent years. Ten years ago, the Chief Charity Commissioner, R.J. Fries, warned the RSPCA that it would be acting in a way inconsistent with its charitable status if it asserted that the infliction of pain on animals could not be justified, even in circumstances in which it confers a higher benefit upon mankind:

> The Commission has not said that the RSPCA may not campaign on animal welfare issues... We have, on the contrary, confirmed that, provided it keeps within our guidelines on political activities and campaigning, it may campaign on these issues. What we have sought to clarify with the RSPCA are the limitations which are imposed on charities which operate in this field and which flow from charitable status, namely that they may not campaign against practices which are to the benefit of human beings even though involving suffering for animals. Any arguments on foxhunting must be based on reasoned argument and evidence, not on the personal viewpoint or emotions of members.[108]

The RSPCA promptly sought a legal opinion on the validity of the ruling, which proved even blunter. 'Charity must serve the overriding object of the public benefit', wrote Christopher McCall QC. 'That is to be measured in terms of the benefit to mankind.'[109] If Ron Kirkby, then chairman of the RSPCA's ruling council, was willing to accept the ruling, Angela Walder, a council member who has been arrested several times for public order offences, preferred a less subservient line. 'We've got little old ladies all round the country giving us money from their pensions to fight for animals,' she said, 'they aren't going to understand this quango saying we can't do it. To hell with the Charity Commissioners.'[110]

It would be interesting to find out what all those little old ladies would make of the fact that, following the publication of a photograph of the Queen strangling a pheasant on a shoot in 2004,[111] Ms Walder tactfully said that having the Queen as a patron was 'like the NSPCC having a paedophile as its patron'.[112] It would also be interesting to know what all those little old ladies would make of the charity's bizarre policy statement that '[w]e believe in the evolutionary and moral kinship of all animals and declare our belief that all sentient creatures have rights to life, liberty and natural enjoyments'[113]—a statement the logical extrapolation of which is the protection of rats, cockroaches and other pests. Such totalising and totalitarian sentimentality, to borrow a phrase from Roger Scruton, gives all charity a bad name.

And it would be interesting, too, to find out what all those little old ladies would make of the charity's use of their pensions for dodgy campaigns. The RSPCA receives almost £90 million a year, entirely from donations and legacies.[114] Not unlike the NSPCC, only half its money is now spent on the inspectorate and on prosecutions. Much of the rest has gone on political campaigns and a £16 million new headquarters.[115] High profile charities like the RSPCA have a duty, not only to animals and donors, but also to other charities, to behave responsibly. A couple of years ago, the APPMWG tried to calculate how much money had been spent on anti-hunting campaigns by the RSPCA, IFAW and the League Against Cruel Sports. It came up with a total of just under £30 million as the expenditure between 1997 and 2002. The RSPCA, it calculated, was responsible for around £15 million. 'Clearly, vast sums of money were spent on the campaign to ban hunting, particularly by the RSPCA.'[116]

Ten years after R.J. Fries's warning, the RSPCA hardly appears to have taken any notice of the Charity Commission's guidance, and the Charity Commission doesn't seem to have the wherewithal to do anything about it. Numerous complaints have been made, but they never amount to anything.[117] And as for the RSPCA, as John Hobhouse has said: 'Those now in charge of the RSPCA should rethink their objectives.'[118]

What can be done about charities like Scope, the NSPCC and the RSPCA? One suggestion is that charity law be modified so that lobbying is done in non-charitable subsidiaries. There are precedents for this in the form of Greenpeace and Amnesty International. Neither is a charity, but both have charitable arms, which perform those purposes of the parent organisations that are charitable. So Amnesty International UK comprises two legal entities: Amnesty International UK Section Ltd and Amnesty International (UK Section) Charitable Trust.[119] The former is responsible for most of the operations carried out in the UK, in particular political campaigning, which is not as a primary activity a charitable purpose. Although its main work of seeking the release of and giving support to prisoners is apolitical anyway, in that it is unbiased, by maintaining the separation of activities it escapes the confusions we have identified in other bodies and places itself beyond reproach. The Charitable Trust is able to carry out those of Amnesty International's purposes which are charitable, such as the relief of poverty for victims of human rights abuse and education and research into human rights abuse.

The advantage of this structural arrangement is that it allows the public to choose whether to give to charitable purposes (which would be eligible for tax relief) or to influence public policy (which would not). It is worth considering whether or not Scope, the NSPCC and the

RSPCA, for example, should be forced to restructure along lines of Amnesty and Greenpeace. As Philip Whittington has argued: 'There are very many kinds of organisation that, through some of their activity, are of great benefit to society, but to which it would be inappropriate to grant tax relief, not least because they are often involved in the controversies of the political domain.'[120]

5

Bureaucracies of Compassion

The rise and rise of supercharities

We have already said that government likes dealing with big charity, but is it possible to quantify the extent to which this is true? That the sector's income is heavily concentrated in a relatively small number of organisations is beyond debate: over two-thirds of the sector's income is now generated by two per cent of the sector's organisations, while at the other end of the scale 87 per cent of the sector's organisations generate less than eight per cent of the sector's income, and all the evidence indicates that this concentration is becoming more acute over time.[1]

The Charities Aid Foundation (CAF), which monitors the top 500 fundraising charities, provides us with the most detailed and accurate data. Not only do donations from individuals, legacies, companies and trusts to the top 1,000 charities now represent over 50 per cent of such donations to all fundraising charities.[2] What is particularly dramatic is that there seems to be a rapidly steepening curve, what mathematicians call a rectangular parabola, across the whole sector, describing a vast rise in total income in the top 500 — even against the next five hundred, namely, numbers 501-1,000. And this trend is becoming increasingly stark. Even in the last year the total income to the top 500 rose from £9.1 billion to £9.7 billion, which represents a 3.8 per cent annual increase, higher even than the year before. By contrast the bottom half of the top 1,000 had an income of only £2 billion.[3]

Figure 5.1
Proportion of Voluntary Income by Centile, with the top ten shown separately, 2004/05

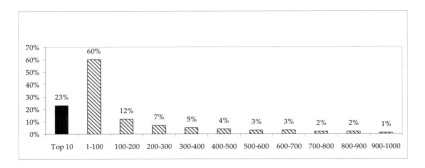

Figure 5.2
Comparison of real-terms annual voluntary income growth rates by centiles, with the top 10 shown separately, 2003/04 - 2004/05

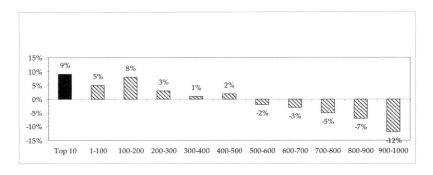

Source: Reproduced from Pharoah, C., Walker, W., Goodey, L. and Clegg, S., *Charity Trends 2006*, London: CAF, 2006, p. 23.

This total income disparity, what CAF describes as a 'huge imbalance of resources between the larger and smaller fundraising charities', derives both from voluntary and non-voluntary income. In terms of voluntary income, of the £5.9 billion donated to the top 1,000 charities, the top 500 attracted £5.3 billion, compared with £670 million amongst the next 500, which represented a robust growth for the top 500 of five per cent on the previous year, as opposed to zero growth in the bottom half of the top 1,000.[4] In terms of statutory income, which is growing at a rate of four per cent annually in the top 1,000, of the £5.7 billion coming in to the top 1,000, £5.3 billion went to the top 500 and just £0.4 billion to the charities in the bottom half of the sample.[5]

If we narrow down the catchment groupings in the top 1,000 to compare the top 100 with the bottom 100, the disparities become even more pronounced. There is a heavy skew in the distribution of income towards the top 100, as the CAF report shows, with their combined voluntary income standing at fifteen times that of the bottom 100. In terms of the share of the overall voluntary income of the top 1,000 the top 100 charities receive 60 per cent, against one per cent in the bottom 100, and the top 10 charities receive one quarter in their own right.[6] There is also a strong and consistent correlation between growth rates and charity size. Figure 5.2 (p. 96) shows that amongst the top centile and the second centile, voluntary income grew considerably faster than amongst all the other centiles. Given the way growth declines down to the bottom 100 charities, this offers over-whelming evidence of the growing dominance of big charities.[7]

If we refine the parameters further to inspect the top 10, the trend towards the concentration of resources in a small number of organisations becomes even more undeniable. The top 10 fundraising charities by total income received £2 billion between them in 2004/05, which accounted for a fifth of the total income to the entire top 500. The dominant position of the top brand name charities is being consolidated, with the same five charities coming top of the table in 2005 as the year before—Cancer Research UK (CRUK), the National Trust, Oxfam, the British Heart Foundation, and RNLI.[8] CRUK remains in a league of is own at the top of the table, both in terms of voluntary and total income, with around twice the voluntary income of its nearest rival, Oxfam.[9]

Table 5.1
Top 10 fundraising charities by total income, 2004/05

Charity	Total income £ m	Ranking by voluntary income in CAF's Top 500
Cancer research UK	384.2	1
Oxfam	253.3	2
National Trust	252.1	3
NCH	207.2	38
Barnardo's	177.4	13
British Red Cross Society	160.3	11
Mencap	157.6	91
British Heart Foundation	144.9	4
Leonard Cheshire	135.1	80
Save the Children (UK)	131.0	10
	2,003.2	

Source: Pharoah, C., Walker, W., Goodey, L. and Clegg, S., *Charity Trends 2006*, London: CAF, 2006, p. 23.

Note: Almost as interesting as the correlation between the top charities by income and the top charities by voluntary income is the disparity between total income and voluntary income for those such as NCH, Mencap and Leonard Cheshire, indicating a disconnect between public support and government support.

Part of the anxiety about the growth of what the NCVO has called 'supercharities'[10] and what CAF calls a 'super-league'[11] derives from our natural affection for small charities in this country. But we need to be careful. In loving the small, we should be wary of automatically lambasting the big, since the assumption, especially but not exclusively in conservative circles, is that small is good, *ipso facto* big is bad.

In fact, there is no need, in praising small charities, to deny the high standard of charitable provision that is, and has for a long time been, characteristic of the likes of the RNLI, the Salvation Army and the National Trust, to name but a few. That said, the evidence suggests, as we shall see, that in some cases big charities have become an instrument of the elites; that professional social workers prescribe politically correct policies; that direct citizen involvement is noticeably reduced; and that they can become commercialised 'entities that rely on mass-marketing techniques to sell a charitable concept to distant, rather uninformed donors'.[12]

What is clear now is that, in general, the bigger big charity gets, the more little charity struggles. As big charity soaks up the cash, little charity is left parched. 'Donations lie at the heart of the voluntary and charitable sector,' as Cathy Pharoah has written, 'expressing direct public engagement in creating and shaping the environment.'[13] Yet in a country of limited resources, these resources are being monopolised by big charities that can capitalise on brand recognition and economies of scale. And it doesn't help when the likes of Martin Narey, the new chief executive of Barnardo's, suggest that the 'Big Five' charities should band together to challenge the government.[14] Bob Holman, an emeritus professor who has worked for many years on Glasgow's notorious Easterhouse Estate, has voiced his suspicion of such 'a top-down approach [that] ignores the advantages of involving locally-run community projects'.[15]

The upshot is that smaller charities can find themselves wedged firmly between a rock and a hard place, unable to attract voluntary donations but discovering, when they turn to the state to safeguard their survival, that they can't compete on a level playing field with the big charities for statutory funding either. This should bother us, for small voluntary and charitable organisations fit our sense of what the sector is all about. To a certain extent this is intuitive—

our fondness for the locally-run and community-based counts for a lot—and any consideration of this can only be insufficiently illustrative of what tens of thousands of small charities do across the country on a day-to-day basis. We should be cautious about asserting the exclusivity of the benefits accruing to any particular kind of organisations, since big charities with effectively scaled operations can, for example, achieve impressive levels of localisation; nevertheless, we can in general say that locally-run community-based projects exhibit certain distinctive qualities.

They are personal. Size is appropriate to the nature and scale of activities. The manager of a day centre, say, can acquire a detailed knowledge of each user that would be much harder in a supercharity. At the Rainbow Trust, a charity which provides flexible practical and emotional help to children with life-limiting conditions and their families, the outreach workers build good relationships with families otherwise neglected by the system, going into their homes and filling a niche which other providers are not well-equipped to offer. The Message Trust has a reputation for quality and innovation, running a wide range of projects in Manchester that place a premium on sustaining relation-ships with young people in disadvantaged local commun-ities. Abbeville's Restaurant in South London, run by the First Step Trust, has a workforce consisting entirely of people with severe and enduring mental health problems. Practical care, not talk about it, has lifted people's horizons —and results in some excellent cooking.[16]

They are responsive. Small agencies are distinctive entities capable of making a contribution disproportionate to their size. Because of their informality, there is space to be flexible and imaginative. One charity that did not want to be named precisely because it has a dedicated donor base and does not seek publicity, and which has for years worked with urban poverty, by, for example, helping women to escape the benefits trap through microcredit schemes, identified a problem with rural poverty and drew upon its private givers for the funding to set up a successful farming distribution network. Honeypot, a charity that runs rural retreats for deprived city children, has the freedom to micromanage its projects as new needs arise, and it maintains that government funding would lead to diminished flexibility. Numerous local charities point out that by being small they can launch new projects if they have a small amount of money and enough willpower and practical expertise— without having to go through the laborious process of bureaucratic review.

They are outside the system. Asylum Aid provides help to asylum seekers who would not approach larger organisations such as the Refugee Council, seeking out vulnerable people unlikely to get help elsewhere through outreach sessions at mental health and HIV clinics.[17] Because its advocates are so involved in the community they are serving, they can identify problems arising long before any government agencies or other bureaucratic organisations could hope to. The Women's Resource Centre is a membership organisation providing support to voluntary and community organisations working to improve the status of women, often working with some of the most marginalised communities in London. As an example, one of its members, the Rape and Sexual Abuse Support Centre, offers confidential face-to-face counselling for women who would not approach more formal and less specialist outfits such as Victim Support.[18] Alternative and innovative, such small bodies can deal with the areas where government fails: there are always going to be people outside whichever system there is, and that's where they operate.

They are effective. Being amateur need not mean being amateurish. Locally-based charities achieve what no amount of paperwork can account for, fostering the close relationships between donors, volunteers and recipients which are so important for a sense of community. Yet they are also often effective in terms of measurable performance. Seventy per cent of cases taken on by Asylum Aid, for instance, are successful at appeal, compared to 20 per cent of cases overall. In 2004, the charity helped over 80 people gain protection at a cost of around £2,700 per case.[19] At the Rape and Sexual Abuse Support Centre, the level of client retention is a useful measure of success, with an impressive average of 85 per cent of clients returning.[20] Furthermore, by seeking to develop close relationships with their donor base, they enter into a more personal level of accountability because private donors want to see their money being spent wisely. In a field where it is often undesirable to even attempt to quantify success, that kind of face-to-face accountability can be better than any amount of targeting and form filling.

The fissuring of the third sector

The changes that are taking place in the voluntary and charitable sector present new and apparently contradictory challenges. Among those who are intimately engaged in the voluntary and charitable sector, it is now widely held that supercharities are coming to resemble the state departments on which they rely for money, not only in size but also in structure and operations. This process has been referred to as isomorphism.[21] With high levels of taxpayers' money in their coffers, for instance, the public has a right to expect of such charities requisite levels of accountability and trans-parency; and as staff numbers and remunerations edge towards professional levels, we have a right to expect a commensurate improvement in efficiency and effectiveness.

Yet, at the same time, there is a growing fraternity of commentators who worry that the very characteristics that we have traditionally associated with the third sector and which make it distinct are being lost or forfeited. We have, first, to ask ourselves if this is how we want things to be. We have, second, to be aware that a chasm has opened up: while some charities have been virtually incorporated into government through their receipt of government funding, and isomorphised to the point of resembling government departments, there are many that remain financially and in every other way independent. Lord Dahrendorf declared in the House of Lords 'that we are in fact witnessing a split in the charity and voluntary sector':

> On the one hand, there is a para-governmental third sector, which is independent in status, but part of the public sphere, notably when it comes to public services. On the other hand, there is still a truly non-governmental sector, which makes no contribution to government-led public policy.[22]

Professionalism and managerialism

Big organisations with big budgets have big workforces. A look at salary and employment reveals just what a super-league the supercharities are in. With average staff numbers of almost 400, and average staff costs of £7.9 million, many of the top fundraising charities are comparable in size to the largest companies in the UK. The paid workforce of the whole sector has grown by almost 10 per cent since 2000, showing that the effects are widespread, but the top 500 account for almost a third of these employees.[23] The largest number of employees employed by a single charity in the top 500 was 6,936: Leonard Cheshire has been the top employer for the last three years and employs six per cent more staff than its nearest rival, NCH, and 10 per cent more than Barnardo's in third place. The National Trust has the highest overall salary bill for any single organisation—£98 million.

The average top salaries for fundraising charities are significantly higher than median chief executive pay in the sector as a whole, which makes it easy to understand why the top charities have become important and attractive employers. The average top salary in CAF's top 500 is £83,000 per annum, a 2.3 per cent increase on last year. The highest salary in the top 500 fundraising charities was £335,000, reported for an employee of the Royal Opera House. Fifty-six of the top 500 charities have employees who earn over £100,000 per annum. The top salaries in fundraising charities were: ROH £335,000, International Planned Parenthood Federation £247,912, Cancer Research £225,000, Institute of Cancer Research £215,000, The National Trust, £195,000.[24]

In the public at large there is some unease about these levels of professionalisation. Polls are notoriously inexact, but they are the only means we have of gauging attitudes. According to a poll by nfpSynergy, over 80 per cent of people think that paying chief executives more than £60,000 may be excessive.[25] However, the realistic, sensible response to this is: sorry guys, get real. It is up to the third sector to do a better job of explaining to the general public why they might be wrong. For if you're going to get someone to run an organisation with an income of over £100 million you're going to need professional managers. You don't want someone with lots of touchy-feely skills and no business sense. You need people experienced at sophisticated accounting, at negotiating through the intricacies of contracts and regulation, at personnel management and firefighting. Competence of this sort costs money.

This is undoubtedly at some remove from the traditional charity in civil society model, but there are many who believe that this is desirable, inevitable and irrevocable. The problem is, the same policymakers who take this line often want to have professionalism while simultaneously maintaining the glowing halo of the committed amateur shaking his tin pot on a windy street. In short, they want to have their cake and eat it:

> The public want to believe that non-profits do good works, are run by nice people in small homely organisations where everybody calls each other by their first names, the sun always shines and they do fantastic work all on a shoestring for little or no pay. Charity marketers want them to go on believing that too. They don't want this rose-tinted view to be shattered because they worry it will impact negatively on fundraising and less measurable types of support. As one colleague said to me, charities should never get 'caught marketing'.[26]

So if the general public are out of touch, if they're naïvely floating around in a rosy fog of ignorance, it may not be their fault. In which case, third sector professionals may be complicit in fudging the issue. This will not do. If the sector is changing, it is the sector's responsibility to communicate to the public how, why, and in what ways. Admittedly, in their different ways the NCVO, ACEVO and the Charity Commission have made diplomatic attempts to encourage this, but too many individual charities are still not making enough of an effort to open up.

The fact is that the greater dependence on contract income, the growing concern of funders to monitor the way in which funding is used, and the growth of consumerist attitudes have all created an environment in which there is ever greater emphasis on the bureaucratic paraphernalia of contract negotiation and management, auditing, accounting and performance reporting. 'The pressure to be efficient, to focus on performance improvement and to win contracts', Ann Blackmore has suggested, 'may cause organisations to employ people with professional and business skills rather than those who are more focused on the actual mission of the organisation'.[27] As one third sector interviewee admitted: 'We are recruiting people from all sorts of backgrounds, for their skills. We are no longer a band of brothers and sisters.

So this is a challenge... the difficulty is instilling our values in new staff—because there are so many new staff.'[28] At its most extreme the consequence is managerialism—managers usurping the role of trustee boards; boards and volunteers becoming less influential than professional staff; and charities focusing on funding and targets rather than on the core mission.

Bureaucratisation

Those who want professionally delivered services should be free to focus on promoting them—on management training, on encouraging performance-related pay, and so on[29]—but we must be aware that this is likely to come at the expense of flexibility and responsiveness. While greater formalisation may encourage greater clarity, it also serves to increase the bureaucratic aspects of the organisation,[30] and 'as the voluntary sector becomes more bureaucratic, and involved in mainstream provision, it is also likely to become less accessible, innovative and diverse'.[31] If this is the case, then the shift towards professionalism and bureaucracy in civil society may be counterproductive.

We might posit a crude continuum: the more bureaucratic, the more sclerotic; the smaller, the more dynamic. It would be the difference between a tugboat and a cruise ship: each has particular qualities, but we have to decide what we want to do what. A senior member of staff at one of the supercharities said that there was no doubting that 'the greater the volume of statutory work you do—and the bigger you are—the less is your ability to innovate'.

When it comes down to it, bureaucracies tend to seek to perpetuate themselves. 'Although these voluntary sector provider organisations may still strive to be innovative and to pilot new patterns of service, their main organisational goal may become organisational survival, with survival to be achieved by receipt of continuing payments for service

106

from statutory organisations.'[32] The director of one charity, in a startling moment of honesty, declared: 'We have an unhealthy relationship with the problem we exist to solve. We should really exist to do ourselves out of a job, but we don't want to be that effective! A lot of nobility is granted — you know, the halo of charity — to what's actually a mucky business.' It is entirely possible that some areas of the sector may start to look like a copy of state bureaucracy — the civil service of civil society.

With the boundaries between public, voluntary and private sectors blurring, public understanding of, and trust in, the voluntary sector are being tested, which places an increasing pressure on organisations to communicate the reality of modern charitable activities. Charities use public money — whether in the form of contracts or simply the tax reliefs which all benefit from — so the public has a right to know how it has been spent. The image of organisations is increasingly connected to their ability to demonstrate value and impact. Fears that trust in charities is declining, driven partly by public reaction to some fundraising practices such as chugging (a contraction of 'charity' and 'mugging', applied to professional street fundraisers, which neatly encapsulates the contradiction), have led to calls for increasing transparency and new mechanisms for account-ability.

This is why such tools as Guidestar have come into being, and why the NCVO launched the ImpACT coalition in the spring of 2006 to campaign for improved transparency about fundraising practices.[33] In addition, NPC and CAF have together launched a couple of funds to allocate money to a portfolio of charities, monitor their impact and keep the donors informed about progress. We have already noted how statutory bodies are keen to audit charitable activity, and in addition both the National Audit Office and the Audit Commission have become increasingly interested in the activities of charities, which is making the quality and robustness of data more and more crucial. 'Regulation of public services', as the NCVO points out, 'is leading to more reliance on performance indicators.'[34]

This also results in competition; and competition, too, as well as transferring funding away from local groups,[35] 'tends to militate against trust'.[36]

Transparency and trust

A charity's assets are not just financial; they are also reputational. That places great responsibility on charities to maintain trust and do everything they can to disperse suspicions of a culture of secrecy. Donors understandably want to know what they are paying for, but according to the head of one major charity—the unattributability of these statements hardly engenders confidence—'if they knew what we actually do they'd stop giving money'. The same goes for charities like the CRAE, and indeed many of the charities mentioned in the previous chapter, who are not exactly transparent about their funding sources. The onus is on charities to say how they are getting and spending, and it should be a requirement of charities to declare clearly how much of their income is made up of statutory funding, whether in the form of grants or fees. Some already do, some don't; all should. The political elites might think that they know better, but the people have a right to be presented with the evidence and make up their own minds.

So public trust depends on the perception of transparency, which for the layman translates into honesty. We have already considered the remuneration of chief executives. A related area of confusion concerns the disbursal of money to different functions within a charity, as we saw with the example of the NSPCC. A recent report by the Centre for Policy Studies (CPS) has exposed how much big charities spend on fundraising and pensions, issues which the Charity Commission's Statement of Recommended Practice (SORP) was introduced to address. SORP guidelines recommend that published figures on paid staff divide them into employment types according to the manner in which the charity's activities are organised. CAF has rationalised this data for the top 500 fundraising charities. It has found that 60 per cent of all staff are employed for 'direct charitable purposes'—that is, active participation in the charity's charitable projects or schemes. In addition, six per cent of all employees are employed mainly in administration, with a further seven per cent being specifically and solely dedicated to fundraising. A further 27 per cent fit into 'other' purposes—a variety of jobs that don't slot into the named categories.[37] But this is still not clear enough.

The first problem category here is staff employed for 'direct charitable purposes'. There remains a perception gap between what the public understand by this and what the third sector professionals mean by this. The Charity Commission, effectively admitting the inadequacies of SORP, wrote in correspondence with the authors of the CPS report: 'The truth of it is that there is no simple definition of what constitutes administration or direct charitable expenditure, and no yard stick applies to all charities.'[38] The second problem category is, of course, 'other'. Whatever constitutes that 27 per cent? It is not the ability to provide clear information but the will to do so that is lacking. For example, the clarity of the annual report and accounts of Sightsavers, the international charity working to combat blindness in developing countries, should make others like the NSPCC ashamed. Sightsavers breaks down exactly where all the money goes, from the different operations in different countries, to the expenditure on employees in different divisions and departments. Is it so much to ask that other charities do the same? Presumably they know for their own purposes, so why the reluctance to come clean?

The public may not be being hoodwinked, but in too many instances charities are hardly going out of their way to tell us what, as donors, it is surely our right to know. When in June 2004 the Charity Commission published a review of the information provided in the Annual Reports and Accounts and Annual Reviews of a sample of 200 of the largest charities—this wasn't SORP but in order to assess the amount of additional information that created a sense of transparency among the charities reporting—the general standards were found to be unsatisfactory. 'Funding bodies and the wider public demand evidence of efficient stewardship of the funds they donate', the Commission declared.[39]

This alone should lead us to expect the burden of transparency and accountability to be greater on bodies with the greatest incomes. Yet there is evidence to suggest that the burden of financial regulation falls most heavily on smaller charities.[40]

The fact is that while the very top charities are successful at attracting both voluntary and non-voluntary income[41]— and the NCVO has predicted that these 'organisations are likely increasingly to shape public perception of the sector as a whole'[42]—smaller charities find it difficult to increase their fundraising capacity and compete for donated income.[43] But if the public wants to see its money spent on beneficiaries rather than more fundraising and publicity, it would do best to give it to small charity. While it costs the average small charity £306.20 to raise £10,000, large charities on average spend £1,071.90 to raise the same amount of money: smaller charities are more efficient at raising money.[44] As we noted with the case of the NSPCC, the danger is that if you are giving to a big charity, you are giving money to help them raise more money, to help them raise more money...

Public trust is not only important because it confers legitimacy on what the voluntary and charitable sector is doing. Very often clients—and the shift away from a model of participatory citizenship, from *beneficiaries* to *clients*, is itself instructive—prefer to use the services of independent voluntary sector organisations rather than state or private sector welfare services because voluntaries and charities are generally trusted more. When this is the case—such as with asylum seekers or abuse victims wanting to stay away from officialdom—we might ask what these clients would think if they knew that the third sector bodies that they were approaching precisely because they were supposed to be at arms' length from the state were really an arm of the state.

Public trust also matters because it leads to the donations, volunteer time and commitment which combine to help the sector to remain independent. For some time it has been observed that as voluntary income declines, the money from local or central government increases, and the reverse is equally true.[45] Evidence from America indicates that when charities receive government funds there is a decrease in private donations.[46] Here, too, '[d]onors are far less likely to support organisations that they perceive to be public sector agencies, and there may be an even greater negative effect if donors become concerned that their time and donations are being used to subsidise those services that they feel should properly be paid for by the state.'[47]

So the charity 'brand' has to maintain its reputation for independence: failing to do so will exacerbate a vicious circle in which the less charities assert their independence the less the public gives them money, and therefore the more they need to turn to the government for funding and support. This is not just about appearing to be independent; it is about demonstrating independence. The Prime Minister's Strategy Unit claims that '[j]ust knowing that an organisation is a charity is often enough to give the public confidence to donate money to it'.[48] Yet while levels of trust and confidence are high, they cannot be taken for granted and there is evidence to suggest that they are being shaken. According to the Association of Charitable Foundations (ACF) Annual Report 2005:

> The public perception of charities is changing, particularly when the charity has a large amount of contract income, and trustees are increasingly wary of making grants to these organisations.[49]

Giving figures

The trends in voluntary donations certainly support these suppositions. We have already noted how a divide is opening up in giving between the supercharities and the rest; that small, expert, user-led organisations which meet local or highly specialised needs, and play a vital role in creating inclusive communities, are struggling to draw support as the big brands dominate the market; and that 'there is a real need to encourage donors in building the resources and capacity amongst the smaller fundraising charities'.[50] But in actual fact, there is a real need to revitalise the whole culture of giving in Britain, since the overall rate of giving is slowing down.

It is virtually impossible to find comparative data for the last hundred or so years, even if logically we might assume that people are less likely to donate voluntarily to causes which they believe the state either should fund, or is perceived to fund, and therefore that with the advent of the welfare state levels of philanthropy would fall. In our pit stop tour of the history of charity we took in one survey conducted in the 1890s which found that the average middle-class family devoted ten per cent of its income to philanthropic works, a larger share than that for any other item except food, but while James Bartholomew attempts to show that giving now languishes at closer to one per cent,[51] the variance in data collection methods alone means that it would be unwise to derive any firm comparative conclusions from these numbers.

Recent trends are more illuminating. Stuart Etherington wrote in 1996 that donations had fallen from 1987 to 1993,[52] and much was made of the dramatic fall in giving that accompanied the introduction of the lottery. It appears that there has been some revival of giving, but while giving is marginally rising as an absolute figure, it is down as a proportion of wealth and down as a proportion of the total money entering the charity sector, taking into account government money.[53] In absolute terms, charitable giving is at its highest levels yet—total individual giving came to £8.2 billion in 2004/05[54]—but in relative terms the picture is far from encouraging: as CAF has found, individual giving as a share of UK GDP has declined over the last decade or so up to 2004/05.[55]

In our attempts to rebuild a culture of philanthropy we might look to America where philanthropy is thriving and where they have never had the same level of government support for social causes: there has never been an expectation that government will provide in the same way. The percentage of individual charitable giving to GDP is more than double in the US what it is in the UK.[56] In 2004/05 it stood at two per cent of GDP, as against the UK where the figure is 0.9 per cent.[57] There are likely to be many reasons for higher US giving. One is sheer tradition: they've always given more. Another is that taxation is lower and the system of tax incentives renders the advantages of giving greater. That is, giving in the US is closely connected to the sense of personal benefit. In a survey published in the *Chronicle of Philanthropy*, 54 per cent of the richest US donors said that they do give for the tax benefit.[58]

The nature of tax incentives needs further consideration in this country, especially given certain confusions that have recently emerged. The Office for the Third Sector (OTS)

Volunteering and Charitable Giving Unit, for instance, is committed to '[e]nabling as many people as possible to give to good causes in a regular and tax-efficient way', and since 2000 the Treasury has played a huge and innovative role in creating a tax regime for giving, taking the initiative in a situation where the Home Office had done nothing for years. However, both schemes are coming into conflict with another Treasury policy, announced in the 2006 Budget, a stringent tightening of the rules to 'counter abuse of charitable reliefs'.[59] Checks and balances are fine, but there is a contradiction at the moment between the drive to encourage donations and monitoring large donors in such a way as to repel big philanthropists.

Perhaps most importantly, Americans seem in general to give more because it makes them feel part of a community. (This is also reflected in the causes they give to—religion and education.)[60] In an 1889 essay entitled 'The Gospel of Wealth', the steel tycoon Andrew Carnegie made a statement that remains influential to this day. He explained that growing inequality was the inescapable price of the wealth creation that made social progress possible. This inequality, however, would undermine the 'ties of brotherhood' that 'bind together the rich and poor in harmonious relationship'. To mitigate the damage arising from this inequality, he argued that the wealthy had a duty to devote their fortunes to philanthropy.[61]

Much energy has been invested recently in encouraging a new generation of philanthropists.[62] The Americans Bill Gates and Warren Buffet represent two of the highest profile converts in recent years, but British donors are also making their mark. As well as high profile celebrity awareness campaigns, the rich have also championed causes which governments seem unable or unwilling to solve. Tom Hunter, for example, teamed up with Bill Clinton to fund the Clinton-Hunter Development Initiative, donating £55 million for African countries' basic needs.[63] It is not just the big givers in America: giving is spread more evenly and regularly across the general public than it is here in Britain. Evidence from the States suggests that the most powerful of the emotions which push people to give is a sense of effective involvement in a charity perceived as doing productive work in a valuable cause.[64]

While it may make economic sense to target wealthier donors and encourage them to give more, there is a need to promote a culture of giving more widely, and recognise giving as an expression of participative citizenship. It is indeed often through giving that people are able to show the concerns, values and beliefs that matter to them. Establishing or strengthening links between giving, volunteering and campaigning will involve providing individuals with a range of opportunities.

The ACF has warned of the 'danger that passion is [being] neutralised': 'People do what they are paid to do rather than what they care deeply about doing.'[65] There has been a strengthening of the power of professionals and full-time workers compared with volunteers. Management has displaced membership and we find ourselves in the curious situation where volunteers are marginalized in voluntary agencies.[66] The supreme paradox is that we have to pay people to volunteer now.[67] Over 50 years ago, Lord Pakenham, a Labour peer and aide to Beveridge, declared that '[t]he voluntary spirit is the very lifeblood of democracy'. He went on: 'We consider that the individual volunteer, the man who is prepared to serve the community for nothing, is he whose personal sense of mission inspires and elevates the whole democratic process.'[68]

Encouraging such voluntarism is complicated by changing social mores—people leading busier lives, greater individualism and commercialism, anxiety about litigation—but what is certain is that it is the job, not of government, but of civil society, where it should reside, to do this. Pointing potential donors to small voluntary and charitable organisations in their local areas offers a way to reconnect people to their communities and revivify our habits of association — and civic democracy.

Changing values

If these small locally-run organisations tend to witness a higher level of donor involvement than supercharities, if they tend to require a different attitude on the part of both recipients and donors because they involve more reciprocal obligations, then they must be at the heart of our vision for a vibrant civil society. Private charity is not about paying taxes and letting 'them' deal with it — whoever 'they' might be — but about personal individual approaches. Such a model promotes cohesion by relying on the ties that bind, what de Tocqueville termed the 'moral tie' between giver and receiver. It is not that big charities and supercharities cannot be personalised in their operations — national and local are not mutually exclusive — but they tend to be less so. The more bureaucratised charities become, and the more integrated into the state, the more we are likely to witness a depersonalisation of charitable action. Whereas government, for example, needs to be and is forceful, coercive, measurable, and so on, it is often right that charity is not, that indeed it is often the opposite, relying on persuasion, on reason, eloquence, and moral values, on beliefs, and helping people to improve their lives.

Where voluntary and charitable organisations develop relationships with organisations from other sectors then they usually start to adopt the approaches of that other sector. This is not necessarily a bad thing — there may well be things that charities can learn from other sectors — but it can be. The concern is that charities may lose their ethos and values, and that what the NCVO has described as:

116

the chaotic, enthusiastic, amateur, volunteer approach will disappear, and along with it the merits of such an approach, such as innovation, flexibility, local involvement and ownership, and the sense that something is done because the people involved care or believe passionately in something. It is argued that this is what is special or distinctive about the sector—what some refer to as 'the magic of charity'.[69]

To return once again to the Community Links report, 'animal farm syndrome' has been identified as the process by which 'voluntary agencies grow and change to look more and more like statutory departments whose function they hope to inherit', with the concomitant 'risk that, in following our enthusiasm for the big public sector contract, third sector organisations will become co-conspirators with government in destroying the very attributes of the sector which, we are both agreed, were precisely the reasons for embarking on this expansionary course in the first place'.[70]

When charities are heavily funded by the state, we are forced to support them. Through taxation we are compelled to pay for something that, since it has not formally been incorporated into government, is not properly within the remit of government. As we have said before, the blurring is the issue. If it's a state department, then it should be acknowledged as such, and funded by the taxpayer in the normal way. But if it's really a quango masquerading as a charity, then it's not really a part of civil society. Those who voice unease are accused of being callous, or simply of whingeing, but charitable activity shouldn't be a statutory duty. If it is any sort of duty, it is a duty of conscience. In the past twenty or so years we have witnessed the rise and rise of bureaucracies of compassion, but as Gertrude Himmelfarb has commented, compassion is a moral sentiment, not a political principle.[71] And as the American political theorist Irving Kristol put it, 'when people start becoming bureaucrats of compassion... then I must say I suspect their good faith'.[72]

There comes a point when a charity stops being a charity, and though it's difficult to say where this point is, a charity that is deriving 90 of its income from statutory sources has surely gone some way past the tipping point. Likewise, along the scale continuum, while there are medium-sized charities, there is nevertheless a category difference between the supercharities and, if not the rest, then certainly the minis. And again, while there are organisations, like Amnesty, that divide their operations between lobbying and campaigning on the one hand and charitable service on the other, a gap is opening up between those with the cash and personnel to fund massive lobbying operations and those who are left to whimper impotently in their photocopied membership newsletters. If we do not want to do away with the big charities, the big lobbying bodies, the big recipients of government money, we will have to make sure that in preserving them we do not make life impossible for the small charities, the charities that prioritise community work, the charities that don't take a penny from the government. This has gone beyond the point of calling for level playing fields. We need to start thinking in terms of different leagues.

6

Nationalised Agencies

A range of borderline and contentious organisational forms now seriously test the definitional frameworks outlined in the first chapter. We can't possibly hope to describe this landscape comprehensively: all that can be done is to point to some striking features. Of the many thousands of organisations that can be added to estimates for the voluntary and charitable sector, a significant proportion—though certainly not all—of these are exempt and excepted charities. Exempt charities are not registered on the grounds that they are regulated by other agencies. Excepted charities are also not registered on the grounds that they are very small organisations with incomes of £1,000 or less, along with certain classes of charity including churches of particular denominations.[1]

Between them, exempt and excepted charities relate to the following areas of activity: recreation—specifically sports clubs (150,000) and social clubs (20,000); culture and arts organisations (30,000); educational organisations (7,000), which are significant in income, expenditure and employment and include approximately 1,500 charitable independent schools,[2] over 5,000 voluntary aided and special schools and grant-maintained schools; housing associations (2,000), which are also significant for other economic indicators; and trade unions, professional and trade associations (3,000). To these can be added community level organisations, which are often transient in nature; associations and self-help groups that are for private benefit but also have a discernible level of public benefit; co-ops and mutuals; community and business enterprises; religious organisations; and registered charities which are arguably part of the governmental apparatus (non-departmental public bodies) and quangos.[3]

The status of some of these bodies is particularly dubious because they are in one way or another nothing other than arms of the state. They have been incorporated. One of the objections to incorporatism presents itself in the form of a paradox: by drawing charities into the apparatus of the state, the state makes them less able to act in the ways that distinguished them as attractive partners in the first place.

Quangos

There is an ever-expanding register of organisations that expose the public benefit test for charitable status as vague, malleable, and vulnerable to anything-goes interpretations. These bodies may in fact be doing good work, but their proximity to government makes it difficult to discern how they can be seen as anything other than non-departmental government bodies. Surviving as they do on involuntary donations in the form of tax, can they also justify receiving the public's freely given donations along with the associated tax advantages?

As we have already noted, the line up for the top 500 fundraising charities—on the whole what people regard as 'charity'—is radically different from the line up of the top 500 charities. As soon as we rank solely according to income and assets, we find a very different pattern emerging. Three examples of major charities will suffice to make a simple initial point: the British Council, the Medical Research Council, and the Arts Council. The British Council is a non-departmental state body. In 2004 £473 million of almost entirely statutory money flushed through its coffers.[4] The Medical Research Council last year had incoming resources of over £518 million, of which at least 82 per cent was government money.[5] The Arts Council, which as anyone who has encountered them will know, gives out money to causes deemed by the government to be worthy, had an income in 2005 of £379 million.[6]

One of the recurrent laments about quangos is their opaqueness. They receive public money but aren't accountable to parliament or the public in any direct way. In the summer of 2006 it was reported that the Baltic Arts Centre in Gateshead had expended £300,000 of public money, given by the Arts Council, on a sculpture by Antony Gormley, who had previously sat on the governing body of the Arts Council, before becoming a trustee on the board at the Baltic Arts Centre—on the recommendation of the Arts Council and Gateshead Council.[7] It is the National Audit Office, which deals with the conduct of state departments, not the Charity Commission, which deals with the conduct of charities, that is investigating accusations of foul play.[8]

In actual fact, however, while these bodies tell us something about the curiosities of what Simon Jenkins has called parastatal charities, they do not illustrate the expansion either of the state into the third sector or of the third sector into the state. They were always both quangos and charities. They are an anomaly and we should bear them in mind. But the real concern of this chapter is with transitional bodies, bodies which once belonged distinctively in one sector or another and which have since changed places.

Stealth taxation

The National Lottery, while not a charity, should prompt some raised eyebrows about the government's attitude towards public money that is supposed to be directed towards charitable causes. It is illustrative of the government's tentacular expansion into regions of public life which were originally pictured as being distinct from the state. The National Lottery was founded in 1994 under the Major government with the explicit aim of raising funds for additional spending on causes and activities that were not covered by the taxpayer.[9] Five good causes were identified: sport, the arts, heritage, charities and projects to celebrate the year 2000 and to mark the beginning of the third millennium. These good causes were each to receive 20 per cent of funding earmarked for good causes (28p in every pound), and each was under the remit of a designated distributing body or bodies.[10] The lottery was to be used 'to restore our heritage, and promote projects which will become a source of national pride'.[11]

However, since 1997 there has been a gradual shift in the use and application of lottery funds. The 1998 National Lottery Act introduced a sixth 'good cause': 'innovative projects in health, education and the environment'. This new 'good cause' was allocated 13.3 per cent of funds.[12] As we will see, this was in stark contrast to the stated aim in 1993 of 'additionality' — that Lottery money would only be used to fund projects that were not covered by the taxpayer and not those that were the province of the Treasury.

The 2006 National Lottery Bill, which received Royal Assent on 11 July 2006, consolidates this use of funds for matters that come under the remit of the taxpayer: the New Opportunities Fund, the vehicle for the distribution of the sixth good cause created in 1998, has been absorbed into a new body, the Big Lottery Fund. This body would absorb 50 per cent of funds earmarked for good causes; the overwhelming majority of which would go to matters previously funded by the Treasury,[13] a manoeuvre which John Major, who was Prime Minister when the lottery was established, has dubbed 'larceny'.[14] All prizes are paid as a lump sum and are tax-free. Of every pound spent on Lottery games, the operating body, Camelot, receives 4.5 pence to cover operating costs and 0.5p profit; 50p goes to the prize fund; 28p to good causes; 12p directly to government; and 5p to retailers as commission.[15]

The main funding bodies are laid out below.

Table 6.1: Distributing bodies set up in the 1993 Act

Good cause (share of funds)	Fund	Distributing body (bodies)
Sport (20 per cent)	Lottery Sports Fund (1994)	• Sports Council (GB) (1972), split into (1997): - UK Sports Council - English Sports Council • Scottish Sports Council (SSC) (1972) • Sports Council for Wales (SCW) (1972) • Sports Council for Northern Ireland (SCNI) (1973)
The Arts (20 per cent)	Funds assigned to the arts	• Arts Council (GB) (1946), split into (1994): - Arts Council of England - Scottish Arts Council - Arts Council of Wales • Arts Council of Northern Ireland (1962)
Heritage (20 per cent)	Heritage Lottery Fund (1994)	• National Heritage Memorial Fund (NHMF) (1980)
Charities (20 per cent)	Funds assigned to charities	• National Lottery Charities Board (1994)
Millennium Projects (20 per cent)	Millennium Fund	• Millennium Commission (1994)

Source: Reproduced from Lea, R. and Lewis, D., *The Larceny of the Lottery Fund*, London: Centre for Policy Studies, January 2006, p. 5.

The National Lottery has come to operate as a stealth tax. Lottery money has become increasingly politicised and is being siphoned off by the government to pay for projects that should be covered by taxation, most notably through the New Opportunities Fund. The New Opportunities Fund 'does not even have the semblance of policy independence...

It is explicitly carrying out government policies, acting in line with the prescriptive "policy directions" set out for it by government.'[16]

Table 6.2: *Distributing bodies set up after the 1998 Act*

Good cause (share of funds)	Fund	Distributing body (bodies)
Sport(16.6 per cent)	Lottery Sports Fund	• UK Sports Council • English Sports Council, rebranded as Sport England (1999) • Scottish Sports Council (SSC), rebranded as Sport Scotland (1999) • Sports Council for Wales (SCW) • Sports Council for Northern Ireland (SCNI)
The Arts (16.6 per cent)	Funds assigned to the arts (including film)	• Arts Council of England, reorganised as Arts Council England (2003) • Scottish Arts Council • Arts Council of Wales • Arts Council of Northern Ireland • Film Council (2000), subsequently renamed UK Film Council • Scottish Screen (1997, distributing lottery funding from 2000)
Heritage (16.6 per cent)	Heritage Lottery Fund	• National Heritage Memorial Fund (NHMF)
Charities (16.6 per cent)		• National Lottery Charities Board, renamed Community Fund (2001)
Millennium projects (20 per cent)	Millennium Fund	• Millennium Commission (ceased receiving funds in August 2001)
Health, education & environment (13.3 per cent)	New Opportunities Fund (1998)	• New Opportunities Fund (created 1998)

Source: Reproduced from *The Larceny of the Lottery Fund*, p. 7.

Table 6.3: Distributing bodies as proposed in the 2006 National Lottery Bill

Good cause (share of funds)	Fund	Distributing body (bodies)
Sport (16.6 per cent)	Lottery Sports Fund	UK Sports Council
		Sport England
		Sport Scotland
		Sports Council for Wales
		Sports Council for Northern Ireland
The Arts (16.6 per cent)	Funds assigned to the arts (including film)	Arts Council England
		Scottish Arts Council
		Arts Council of Wales
		Arts Council of Northern Ireland
		UK Film Council
		Scottish Screen
Heritage (16.6 per cent)	Heritage Lottery Fund	Administered by the National Heritage Memorial Fund (NHMF)
Charities and health, education & environment (50 per cent)	Big Lottery Fund	In June 2004 the Community Fund and the New Opportunities Fund merged administratively to form the Big Lottery Fund. They are still separate legal entities
Millennium projects (0 per cent)		Millennium Commission

Source: Reproduced from *The Larceny of the Lottery Fund*, p. 12.

What's more, the quangos set up to administer lottery money are now subject to government monitoring and guidelines: following the 1998 National Lottery Act, the distributing bodies have now to construct strategic plans in line with government policies, and are now *de facto* delivery arms of government policy, funded through the lottery.[17] Magnus Linklater, writing in *The Times* in 2004, commented

that 'a growing proportion of [lottery money] is channelled
to projects which are either approved of or positively
insisted on by government'.[18] A good example of this came
with the rejection in 2005 of a grant for the Samaritans in
Sheffield on the grounds that it was not doing enough for
the disadvantaged, asylum seekers and ethnic minorities—
even though the Samaritans have no control over who calls
them up.[19] This is the way with this government: it speaks of
diversity but seeks to make everything in its own image.

The 2006 National Lottery Bill, going through the House
of Lords at the time of writing, will give the government
even more say over the distribution of lottery funds. The
formation of the Big Lottery Fund is the most egregious
example of government interference in the Lottery. Already
the biggest single charitable grantmaker in the UK,[20] the Big
Lottery Fund is slated to take up fully 50 per cent of total
lottery funds, and as much as 40 per cent of that could be
spent on policy initiatives in health, education and the
environment. Traditional good causes will increasingly be
marginalised. The NCVO, which expresses 'concern over the
principle of additionality', warns of the possibility of 'a
reduction in money for less well-known causes'.[21] What's
more, with the 2012 Olympic games coming to Britain, an
estimated £1.5 billion is being diverted from good causes to
pay for this:[22] £750 million is to be raised through scratch-
cards, while the remaining £340m of lottery funding is to
come from the Sports Lottery Fund, and, if necessary, up to
£410m from mainstream lottery games from 2009. This was
confirmed by Tessa Jowell.[23]

In this way the distinction between public spending and
lottery grants has been lost, and the National Lottery can
now legitimately be seen as a stealth tax. The public have
not been consulted on this shift of emphasis for Lottery
spending; while being assured that their money goes to
good causes, it is now being diverted from its original

purpose to the Treasury, in order to shore up shortfalls in health and education spending. While it is hard to argue against improved treatments for heart patients, that is not what the lottery was set up to achieve and that is not where people expect their lottery cash to be going. So when charities in receipt of significant sums of money from the lottery use it as evidence of their independence from government-disbursed funds, the bald truth is that they're either kidding themselves or being disingenuous.

Changing places

In the kinds of charities which have already been examined in some detail—charities which have even in recent times been entirely funded by the public—a debate rages as to whether or not the government is encroaching on the space that properly belongs to the voluntary and charitable sector or whether the sector is moving—or being moved—into the space that should be occupied by government.[24] In a sense it is immaterial in which direction the movement is happening if the sum effect is an attenuation of the gap between the two sectors. However, there are a few organisational forms where the direction of movement, as it were, can be easily discerned. On the one hand, for instance, there are statutory bodies which have been turned into charities—leisure trust transfers—and on the other hand, there are charities which have been acquired wholesale by the state—such as housing associations. We need to examine both to get a clearer sense of how the changes are occurring.

Local authority trusteeships

The Charity Commission warns that 'increased co-operation increases charities' reliance upon the state for fundraising and, in turn, creates a potential risk to charities' inde-pendence'.[25] This is troublesome territory, however, since government authorities are permitted to set up charities, provided that the purposes are exclusively charitable. It is also possible for charitable purposes to coincide with government functions. Yet this comes with a proviso or caveat: it is possible that 'a body may be created with a stated purpose that is charitable, but with an unstated purpose that is concerned with giving effect to the wishes and policies of a government authority'.[26] According to the Charity Commission, in this case:

> It would be difficult to avoid the conclusion that a body of that kind was not really a charity at all. Instead of being set up for the stated charitable purpose, it would exist in fact for the purpose of securing the benefits of charitable status while carrying out the wishes and policies of the governmental authority. In that case, the body would not be a charity because it would not have been established for purposes that are exclusively charitable.[27]

Trustees should be independent, too, and yet it has been confirmed that there are 731 charities which have a local authority as a trustee. Moreover, in 595 of these bodies, the local authority is the *sole* trustee.[28] Writing for the *Guardian* in 2006, Rosie Chapman of the Charity Commission said that trustees 'co-opted by public authorities can forget which hat they are wearing and need to be reminded'.[29]

Paddington Recreation Ground is a charity which has a local authority—in this case Westminster City Council—as its sole trustee. In 2003, the charity had an income and expenditure of £885,000. This money was raised almost exclusively from the state as fees for the operation of the recreation ground, with only about £5,000 coming from miscellaneous commercial activity and none from direct donation.[30] The address for correspondence with the charity is registered with the Commission as that of the Director of Legal Services at Westminster City Hall. The address of their website, also registered with the Commission, is the home page of Westminster City Council.

The authors of the CPS report investigated this outfit. On interviewing a spokesman for Westminster City Council, they learned that there had in recent years been a strategic decision to keep the Paddington Recreation Ground as a charity. This spokesman explained that the main reason for the local authority wanting Paddington Recreation Ground to retain its charitable status was the relief it would continue to enjoy from taxation. Were it administered as a part of the City Council, it would be liable for a series of levies. The spokesman even admitted that 'third parties might be persuaded to give to a charity, but they would never give to a local authority'.[31]

Given the Charity Commission's guidelines on trustee-ship, it is difficult to see how the Paddington Recreation Ground can be said to fulfil the criteria for a charity. Such a state-owned and state-run entity is not in any traditional understanding of the term operating in the public benefit. It should therefore be deregistered as a charity and enter into the wider voluntary sector. There is no question that it undermines the charity brand, and the public would be right to regard such dealings with a due amount of suspicion. In fact, it is not just that local authorities should not be allowed to be the sole trustee of a charity: they should not, because of the conflicts of interest that inevitably arise, be trustees at all.

Leisure trust transfers

A 40 per cent increase in the number of general charities since 1995 masks a much bigger increase in the number of large charities. Those with incomes of over £1 million have more than doubled in the last decade, as a result of both organic growth (small charities getting bigger) and the inclusion of new entrants into the sector that began life with significant resources. While some of these new entrants reflect significant new resources coming into the sector, such as new charitable foundations, others reflect what the NCVO terms the 'charitisation' of the public sector.[32] A crucial example is the emergence of new leisure trusts. These new entrants made a significant contribution to the increase in the sector's income of just over £1 billion from 2002/03 to 2003/04.[33]

The Charity Commission's guidelines on the independence of charities from the state point out that 'a local authority could not expect simply to convert its leisure department into a charity. Nor could it create as a charity a body whose purpose was to carry out the local authority's leisure policies or to participate in whatever recreational initiatives the local authority decided upon from time to time.'[34] This seems unequivocal. Yet in January 2005, the Commission decided that both the Trafford Community Leisure Trust (TCLT) and the Wigan Leisure and Culture Trust (WLCT) were entitled to be registered as charities under law.[35] In considering the applications from TCLT and WLCT to register as charities, 'the Commission concluded that the law does not prevent charities from using their own funds to provide services on behalf of public authorities, even if an authority has a legal duty to provide a service. The Commission recognised that in practice a number of charities were already doing this to some extent.'[36]

So the Commission's decision was essentially based on the logic that if everyone's doing it we might as well make it legal. If you can't beat them, join them. As for the idea that these charities are using their own funds to provide services on behalf of public authorities, that beggars belief. Such a body is not using its own funds to provide services on behalf of public authorities, but is vestigially a public authority body, with its income solely derived from statutory sources, doing what it did when classified as a local authority administered leisure centre, only now enjoying the benefits of charitable status. In both instances the major funder is the local council, although some other income flows from other statutory sources.[37] These leisure trust charities do not own their assets, they merely lease them from councils under partnership contracts.

At least 99 per cent of the income at the WLCT derives from statutory funding.[38] One thing is certain: these hybrids are unlikely to benefit in any way from philanthropy. Who, seriously, is going to voluntarily donate their money to the local authority swimming baths? Have no fear: the Commission's got that one sorted too. The Commissioners note—and this is flabbergasting—that 'it was accepted as a good charitable purpose to relieve the community from general or local taxation provided that such purpose was applied for the benefit of a sufficient section of the community'.[39] So not only has 'public benefit' been stretched to accommodate leisure centres, but, however this statement is read, taxation or the relief of taxation has now become 'a good charitable purpose'. You don't need to be a soothsayer to see that it's only a matter of time before central government departments are being granted charitable status.[40]

It's worth bearing in mind, too, that now these leisure trusts are charities they are able to receive National Lottery funding. Genuinely deserving voluntary and charitable organisations will, of course, lose out as National Lottery funds are directed by the government into government repositories. Quite apart from the likelihood that this move could damage donations to legitimate causes, proper charities find themselves up against unfair, subsidised competition. This sleight of hand lets the state off the hook of its legal duties and allows councils to make concealed cuts through the cheap and cheerful charity route. And all for the public benefit. According to the decision document, the local authorities are to 'monitor' the funding of the two trusts, and the boards of trustees are to be carefully selected to ensure that there are no potential conflicts of interest.[41] No potential conflicts of interest? Some hope.

Housing associations

Today's housing associations derive from the nineteenth-century housing societies, with an important difference. When philanthropists began to turn their attention towards the issue of providing decent housing for working-class people in the early part of the nineteenth century, it was taken for granted that no subsidy should be involved. To provide a 'necessary of life' such as housing at a subsidised price would be to turn the recipient into a second-class citizen, unable fully to participate in society. The progenitors of those early housing charities spent days and nights struggling to find ways of providing accommodation for low-income tenants at rents that would cover the capital costs and show a modest return on the investment. It became known as 'philanthropy and five per cent', although some of the charities accepted a lower return on their capital; the Peabody Trust, for example, required three per cent.

The 1890 Housing of the Working Classes Act, which allowed local authorities to borrow money to buy land and build housing, saw the first significant incursion of the state into this field of what is now called social housing. Octavia Hill, the fiercely anti-statist housing reformer, warned of the fall-out from such an expansion of the powers of local government: local authorities would make bad landlords because their tenants would be their voters, so there would be a disincentive to pursue bad payers and punish anti-social behaviour; the huge sums of money involved would bring corruption into local government; and worst of all, they would be able to use their access to public money to undercut the market, creating an unfair competition with housing charities (whose rents had to cover actual costs) and forcing ratepayers—including some of the respectable poor living in charitable schemes—to subsidise their feckless neighbours.

She turned out to be right on every count. Subsidised rents made 'philanthropy and five per cent' impossible. Rents could no longer be set at a realistic level. Nor would it be possible to insist on high standards of behaviour when tenants who were pressured could simply move into local authority accommodation and live as drunk as lords undisturbed.

Housing charities found themselves in the same difficulties as other sectors that experienced an incursion by the state into their territory. This crisis was particularly acute for housing charities, as they had not been in the business of soliciting donations: their capital was provided by share-holders, who were paid dividends out of the rents. If rents no longer could be set at a level that covered costs—because they were competing with local authority rents—how could they survive? As the twentieth century progressed, many housing societies closed or merged, although some, especially the larger operators, continued to fulfil a role in spite of a degree of regulation—in terms of fixed rents and secure tenancies—that no other part of the voluntary sector had to contend with. Housing charities, unable to operate in the way they had developed in the nineteenth century, came to rely on state subsidies, just like local authority housing providers.

Crucially, subsidies made it possible for the state to incorporate, rather than displace, housing charities. In 1964-66 the Labour government set up the Housing Corporation, but the great period of expansion began with the 1974 Housing Act, which introduced a capital subsidy to registered social landlords (RSLs) of up to 100 per cent, known as the Housing Association Grant.[42] This was ratcheted up when Margaret Thatcher's Conservative government decided to 'shrink' the public sector by handing

over contracts to housing associations—supposedly representing the voluntary and charitable sector—to build and
run social housing. Many local authority estates were
transferred *en bloc* to housing associations, some of which
had been set up specially to receive them. This crude sleight
of hand allowed the government of the day to claim that the
state sector was being reduced, in spite of the fact that
housing associations received huge grants of public money
via the Housing Corporation, and in many cases the tenants'
rent was paid by housing benefit—another Conservative
innovation.

Table 6.4

*Actual total central government funding, non-housing association funding and
housing association funding of voluntary and community organisations in the
UK, 1999/2000 to 2001/02 at constant (2000) prices (£)*

	Actual non-housing association funding (£)	Actual housing association funding (£)	Actual total funding (£)
1999/2000	1,049,461,972	1,220,718,578	2,270,180,550
2001/2002	1,988,591,708	1,260,390,589	3,248,982,297

Source: Mocroft, I. and Zimmeck, M., *Central Government Funding of Voluntary
and Community Organisations 1982/83 to 2001/02*, London: Home Office, 2004,
p. 4.

The extent to which the voluntary housing sector has
been colonised by the state is easy to illustrate by the
enormous injections of government funding into housing
associations. Indeed, housing association funding is the
largest single component of central government funding to
the third sector. In 1999/2000 it accounted for 53.8 per cent of
total funding to the third sector, and although that proportion has been decreasing, that is because of the rapid
hiking of the totals invested in non-housing association
causes.[43] In 1999/2000, non-housing association funding

stood at approximately £1 billion and housing association funding at £1.2 billion. By 2001/02, non-housing association funding had doubled to £2 billion and housing association funding had increased marginally to £1.3 billion.[44] If it has not already become so, the housing association sector seems set to become the second largest tenure category (after owner occupation) within the next few years.[45]

Not surprisingly, housing associations have found that public money brings with it a measure of political control. Regulation has led to coercive isomorphism, since in order to secure public subsidy, housing associations were required to conform with a prescriptive regulatory regime operated by the Housing Corporation.[46] 'In the past voluntary board members were often responsible for raising development capital and they were genuinely accountable to their shareholders (who were major financial stakeholders),' Peter Malpass of the University of West England has argued, 'but now the financial, administrative and strategic framework is such that boards have been reduced to a largely symbolic position, providing a figleaf to cover the fact that the real power lies elsewhere, with financial institutions, the local authorities, the Housing Corporation and the government.'[47] This has brought 'both a loss of accountability at the local level and an increase in the power of the centre.'[48]

One major problem concerns the nomination of tenants. Most of the social housing providers of the nineteenth century were precise and selective about whom they wanted to accommodate: the respectable working poor. But soon housing associations in receipt of statutory funds found that they were expected to take a percentage of tenant nominations from the local authority as a *quid pro quo*. In 1995, the Audit Commission declared that about 60 per cent of housing associations' new tenants (excluding transfers) were nominated by local authorities.[49] That figure is almost certainly much higher now, and in some cases it is 100 per cent. The Charity Commission is clear in its guidance for RSLs that they should be independent of other bodies, and 'have the final choice over all tenants (beneficiaries)'. It goes on to state that 'there can be no question of any outside body having a right of selection, only a right to nominate candidates for consideration by the RSL'.[50] In practice, however, the local authority does virtually have a right of selection concerning people seeking re-housing.

A recent report by the charity Shelter, for example, which examined the collaboration between local authorities and RSLs, states that '[t]he Corporation *expects* RSLs to provide a reasonable proportion of their housing stock to LA's nominations. The corporation *expects* RSLs to demonstrate their cooperation with LA homelessness reviews and strategies and in the delivering of LA homelessness functions.'[51] It is difficult to sustain an interpretation of this other than one which arrives at the conclusion that RSLs are carrying out activities that further the purpose of a non-charitable body. So housing associations have found themselves performing a role that is indistinguishable from that of local council housing departments. They are funded and regulated by the government, and few residents of social housing distinguish between social housing managed directly by the local authority, and that managed by a housing association or registered social landlord which they have been allocated via the local authority housing list.[52]

Those at the top of the housing list must be offered the first suitable property that becomes available, and an applicant's position on the list is determined by 'housing need', which is a political construct: it reflects a combination of the local authority's priorities and its statutory responsibilities laid down by parliament. In practice this means that units are allocated to homeless persons, lone parents and the economically inactive before they are offered to working families. The problem this creates is that housing associations end up with high concentrations of multiple-needs households, which in turn create estates with unmanageable social problems. There is also considerable anecdotal evidence to suggest that councils 'dump' their most troublesome tenants on housing associations, turning them into sink estates. As a Joseph Rowntree study found some years ago, 'the social and economic base of the sector is becoming ever narrower... These trends make it harder to sustain stable communities.'[53]

What's more, housing associations receiving Housing Corporation funding are under such pressure to take whichever tenants are proposed by their local authority housing department that some of them no longer even bother to keep their own waiting lists. The Octavia Hill Housing Association—the direct descendent of Octavia Hill's own Horace Street Trust founded in 1886—closed down its own list in the 1980s in favour of taking local authority nominations, which is particularly ironic given that Octavia Hill herself regarded the careful choice of tenants as a key element in housing work.

For the purposes of our inquiry, it is useful to look at how this development has come about through the lens of one of the biggest of the housing associations, the Peabody Trust. The Peabody Trust was established in 1862 by the wealthy American anglophile George Peabody with an original grant of £150,000 which was increased to £500,000 by the time of his death. Peabody believed that the poor should only be helped in ways which encouraged independence. 'The self-reliance and honest independence of the working poor,' he told an audience in the Guildhall in 1866, 'are the best guarantee of a country's prosperity and moral greatness.'[54] The first Peabody Buildings opened in Spitalfields in 1864, followed by Peabody Square in Islington in 1865. Soon the volume of units of accommodation provided all across London was immense. By 1882—by which time there were

also hundreds of other associations of all shapes and sizes—
Peabody owned 3,500 dwellings housing more than 14,600
people.[55]

The Peabody Trust is one of the few nineteenth-century
housing charities that not only survived the entry of the state
into the sector, but learned to go with the flow, and has
flourished accordingly. It is now enormous, with 17,230
properties across 27 London boroughs, but it finds itself in
something of a quandary. A recent Audit Commission
report on the Trust was damning. It said there was 'scope for
considerable improvement' and found that 'the Trust's
performance is unimpressive compared with its peer
group'.[56] Yet the fact is that the Trust is forced to deal with
high levels of 'nuisance' and antisocial behaviour,[57]
presumably largely from tenants it would not—because the
original object of the charity was the provision of housing
for 'artisans' and the 'deserving poor'—otherwise have to
accommodate. Many other housing associations also
struggle with such deflated social capital. A resident survey
at another housing association revealed a distinctive feature
of such estates: 'Sixty-eight per cent of residents reported
that they thought the estate was getting worse, 74 per cent
responded that drug or alcohol abuse was a major problem,
and 60 per cent would not recommend living in the area to a
friend.'[58]

The lack of personal responsibility among the tenants is a
reflection of the lack of responsibility among management.
For the social problems are compounded by management
from afar in remote housing association central offices with
housing officers rarely visiting their properties. Lacking
clarity of responsibility, many of the associations will not
respond to residents behaving anti-socially within their
neighbourhood. It is not even seen as a local authority
problem, so there is a lack of adequate oversight of the
whole area. With such a lack of engagement between tenants

and management, and the low levels of participation and satisfaction among tenants reported by a House of Commons Committee,[59] vicious circles, not virtuous circles, are here to stay. Housing associations now exacerbate what they were established to alleviate.

Many, like the Peabody Trust, despite their chequered record, have become massive in recent years, reflecting disparities shared with the wider voluntary and charitable sector. Their strength in securing finance has led to the formation of a 'super-league of large, regularly developing associations' which, because of 'the pressures of competition', have come to 'operate in a defensive and non-collaborative environment'.[60] Most no longer have recourse to volunteers, nor is there much voluntary funding. They pay their board members—which is extremely rare for registered charities—and many of their chief executive officers are paid extraordinary sums for the charity sector— even against the pay packages received by the heads of some of the biggest recognised charities (the median in 2003 was roughly £100,000, with a number rising over the £200,000 benchmark).[61] All of which, in terms of ethos, structure and funding, is quite at odds with the spirit of the voluntary sector. 'The very large associations that dominate the sector have been transformed into social businesses with little claim to be voluntary organisations.'[62] Housing associations are exempt charities. They should be excised charities. Excised, that is, from the charity register.

7

Where Do We Go From Here?

Change is inevitable; progress is not. In examining a wide range of issues pertaining to the voluntary and charitable sector, asking all along what is the essence of such organisations, and how they are being threatened and encouraged in their work, the spirit of the inquiry has been more diagnostic than didactic. Now the time has come to make some tentative suggestions for reform—not outright solutions but matters for discussion—in order to enhance the reputation and effectiveness of the sector. Two broad recommendations are made: firstly, that we seek, not to widen the definition of charities to nothing more rigorous than the public benefit test, but rather to clarify the distinctions between different types of organisation; and secondly, that we search for ways to bolster the independence of genuine voluntary and charitable organisations by nominating guardians of independence.

Differentiation

Greater differentiation within the sector is required. This will not be easy, but an image marshalled by the philosopher Ludwig Wittgenstein may give us hope. He asks us to consider a lamp in a dark room: it casts a circle of light, around which is a grey transitional zone and a region of darkness beyond. Though it is difficult to state precisely where the light begins and ends it is still possible to say that there are areas wholly within the glare of the lamp and areas wholly without. One need not say that everything is grey just because it is hard to draw firm lines.

Earlier in the book we noted that if definitions seek to find attributes that organisations share, classifications seek to find attributes that separate them. This is a difficult and potentially technical business. Distinctions will be subject to criticism wherever they are set, and some might counter that this is an arbitrary exercise, but we have to make a start. The current situation cannot be sustained. We have to find ways to clarify the difference between service providers, local voluntary bodies and campaigning and lobbying bodies; between charities that are independent of the state and those that are more like quangos and non-departmental government bodies; and between fundraising bodies and those that currently engage in little or no fundraising.

Size

Since there is widespread anxiety about the way that supercharities are having an adverse effect on small charities, one way forward would be to distinguish them separately under law. Although some of the supercharities don't get much state funding, we have noted how many of them do; and even those that don't can make life hard for their smaller relatives in the sector. It is difficult to see what a small local voluntary body, a soup kitchen or micro-credit finance scheme, for instance, has in common with a multi-million pound organisation like Barnardo's or Leonard Cheshire. There are service-providing charities that can provide innovative approaches and those that aren't innovative but that can arguably provide an equally important service. There are those that depend largely on volunteers and those whose workforce is mainly paid, and therefore by definition not voluntary.

When they are both bidding for contracts, or soliciting the general public's donations, there is no hope of them currently competing on a level playing field. They should therefore be officially recognised as belonging to different

141

leagues. Big charities over a certain threshold should be subject to increased regulations and imposed best practice; while small charities under a certain threshold should be protected from over-regulation. Gradations at different thresholds would be an option.

The Strategy Unit has recommended that big charities (income of £1 million plus) should have to fill out a Standard Information Return. This requires that big charities have expenditure broken down in audited accounts and presented in a common format. It builds on SORP, to include improved methods for apportioning costs and expenditure, enabling more meaningful financial comparisons between organisations to be made.[1] It recommends a lower level of regulation for charities with an income between £10,000 and £1 million—that they have their accounts examined by an independent person.[2] Those below £10,000 are considered to have the least regulatory risk and limited capacity to deal with regulation.[3] Below the £10,000 mark a charity would still have to send accounts to anyone who asks and could still be investigated if improper activity of any sort were reported. These should, the Strategy Unit suggests, be called 'Small Charities'.[4]

The general division is to be endorsed, but the levels should be set differently. In order to make a clearer division between the small, medium and large, the levels could be set at £10,000, as suggested, and £1 million, but in addition a new threshold should be set at £100 million. This would create four categories according to size: small, medium, large and supercharities. Those above £100 million would be subject to the strictest transparency and accountability requirements. For example, donors should be entitled to know exactly how much money will go on fundraising, how much on lobbying and campaigning, how much on service delivery, and so on. Supercharities should list numbers of employee by job description—from senior management and business administrators, to public relations officers, in-house and contracted lobbyists, practical workers, street collectors and volunteers, and so on.

The fact is that if bodies are to benefit from tax advantages, and from the reputational advantages associated with charitable status, they must accept the associated responsibilities. The NCVO's ImpACT (Improving Accountability, Clarity and Transparency) Coalition talks of promoting the message that charities are effective and do a great job, that charities use donations carefully and wisely, that charities are highly regulated and adhere to a range of strict standards.[5] The challenge will be to make sure that transparency does not mean merely a *display* of transparency. This should not be a public relations exercise but a concerted effort to improve the sector's accountability, clarity and transparency. Structural changes in the sector would be a step in the right direction.

Funding

Before we say anything else, there should be a far greater stress on something that is already touted as best practice — the diversification of income streams — than there is at present. The Charity Commission recommends it, as does the NCVO, but no one seems willing to arraign those who become overdependent on a single (and in this investigation we really mean public) source. Full-cost recovery, as well as various other sensible guidelines for those who enter into contracts with the state, needs to become a reality — and soon. As a minimum requirement, all charities should be required to declare as a matter of course the proportion of their income derived from all statutory sources, both in grants and contract fees. The disingenuousness of those charities spoken to during the course of researching this book who quoted their grant income but not their contract income should be prohibited.

What about the colonising of the voluntary and charitable sector by the state? It may not be desirable, let alone practical, for the voluntary and charitable sector, or society as a whole, to call for the withdrawal of all state funding. Although a number of the big charities claim that they would be able to survive without the massive influx of statutory grants and contract fees—in which case they should probably be encouraged to do so—the idea that those charities receiving 80 or 90 percent of their income from the state could survive without it seems like wishful thinking. As Richard Kramer, director of policy at the charity Turning Point, which receives 96 per cent of its annual income from statutory agencies, said recently: 'If Turning Point's funding from local authorities and primary care trusts was arbitrarily stopped the effect would be felt by the 130,000 clients we support, leading to the closure of our treatment services for drug and alcohol misusers, [and] withdrawal of our support for people with severe mental health problems and learning disabilities.'[6] Polly Toynbee has also argued that this would create a void that nothing could fill, and it is difficult to disagree.[7] If we truly care about the 'clients' of these big charities then we cannot advocate policies that penalise them. We do not want to create any more instability in the sector than already exists. This does not, however, mean that things are satisfactory as they stand.

We have to stress the distinctions between bodies that receive the majority of their funds from the government and those that don't. As CAF says, '[t]here is an urgent challenge for social care charities... to make clear the right balance between private and state income. Some charities raise increasing levels of donations for services which could be perceived as a government responsibility.'[8] Charities receiving no money from the state, and especially those heavily dependent on volunteers, should be encouraged in that course by receiving the greatest tax advantages: that is, they should be encouraged to avoid state funding by receiving commensurate benefits. Small charities that get no government money should be outside the regulatory reach of government. Big charities that get no money from the government would be entitled to the tax advantages but they would be regulated on the basis of their size, as outlined above.

For the rest, thresholds could be set relating to state funding. As we saw in chapter 3, charities very often justify the money they take from statutory sources on the basis of tipping points. So some take nothing, of course; the Catholic Children's Society takes 30 per cent, above which it believes it would compromise its independence; Save the Children talk of 50 per cent as the limit, above which they would lose their autonomy; and others like Barnardo's appear to set their limits, for the time being, at 78 per cent, or 88 per cent, or 96 per cent... Since the levels of state funding are often set arbitrarily, there is a case for trying to organise charities into different categories along the principle of Wittgenstein's lamp: two distinct regions—the light and the dark—along with a transitional zone.

We could posit two thresholds—at 30 per cent and 70 per cent of gross income. Charities receiving less than 30 per cent of their income from the state and its agencies could still benefit from the advantages that charitable status currently affords. Those receiving between 30 and 70 per cent of their income from the state and its agencies could be called state-funded charities and benefit from more modest tax concessions. This new category would effectively go some way towards reflecting the particularity of charity under law as opposed to the more general voluntary sector, positioning them somewhere in the hinterland between registered charities and voluntary organisations (though admittedly this does not resolve the confused meanings of the word 'voluntary'). Those bodies getting the vast majority of their funding from the state—above 70 per cent—are already *de facto* state agencies, or quangos, or satellites, and it is time that that relationship was formalised. They could still receive that money from the government, but they couldn't still be considered charities.

These categories would present charities that have allowed themselves to drift with some stark decisions—decisions which they should have been making more consciously or strategically than they perhaps have been to date. As things stand, a number of the biggest brands, such as Barnardo's, NCH and Leonard Cheshire, would find themselves in an uncomfortable position. As for state payrolled housing associations and leisure trusts, which are entirely funded by statutory bodies and make a mockery of the Charity Commission's guidance on independence from the state, they should be officially transferred to the state sector and lose their charitable status. The Chancellor's announcement about an Office for the Third Sector could concern itself with those bodies which are still charities but which come within its remit as State-funded charities.

In this way we would be able to clarify what truly resides in the third sector.

Table 7.1

Hypothetical breakdown of charities qualifying into new categories

Classification	Example charities
Independent charities (receiving less than 30 per cent of their income from the state)	NSPCC National Trust RNLI The Salvation Army
State-funded charities (receiving between 30 and 70 per cent of their income from the state)	Save the Children Oxfam Shelter British Red Cross
Statutory agencies (receiving 70 per cent or more of their income from the state)	Turning Point NCH Barnardo's National Family and Parenting Institute

Political activity

The principle of clarity in classification should again be uppermost. It is a cause for concern that so many charities, both funded and not funded by government, have become so active in lobbying and campaigning along political lines. The case reaches its most absurd when the government is paying charities to tell it what to think. These bodies are little more than statutory agencies and the above distinctions would apply to them. We have a responsibility to consider not just individual cases, but the charity brand in general, and political activity runs counter to the Charity Commission's guidelines and erodes public confidence. For a start, there is a need for clearer guidance on advocacy, campaigning and lobbying; and strict best practice guidelines on what is acceptable and what is not should be enforced.

If lobbying is here to stay, how can we clear up the shadiness that surrounds it? One way would be to make a clear distinction between bodies that engage in such activities and bodies that don't and primarily concentrate on delivering services. Some charities argue that lobbying is important to further their purposes; and it would perhaps be unduly punitive to force charities into a binary choice between being either the one type or the other. However, if no alterations are made to the status quo then there will be no way of preventing charities from becoming primarily or even entirely politicised lobbying and campaigning organisations; and worse, of government funding these organisations to engage in often politically controversial operations.

One suggestion is that charity law be modified so that lobbying is done in non-charitable subsidiaries, as is the arrangement for Greenpeace and Amnesty International. The advantage of this structural arrangement is that it allows the public to choose whether to give to charitable purposes (for which they are eligible for tax relief) or to influence public policy (for which they are not). There are very many kinds of organisation that, through some of their activities, are of great benefit to society, but to which it would be inappropriate to grant tax relief, not least because they are often involved in the controversies of the political domain.

It is right that charities go upstream, in William Booth's words, if campaigning in the public domain for non-political ends fits their charitable objects. But the behaviour of the RSPCA, or of some of the more politically aligned coalitions, does not fit this ideal, and we need provisions to prevent abuse of charities' privileged status. In the end we could posit four categories:

- Lobbying and campaigning organisations—including politically aligned and motivated groups—that are not charities

- Charities that do not lobby and campaign

- Organisations that are divided into a charitable arm and a campaigning arm

- Lobbying and campaigning coalitions that represent charities but aren't charities themselves.

The guardians of independence

Trustees

Although the Strategy Unit acknowledged that 'there is little evidence that the promise of payment is an effective general incentive to take on trusteeship',[9] it also asserted that 'a trustee should be allowed to be paid for a service if the trustee body, as a whole, reasonably believe it to be in the charity's interests that the service should be provided by the trustee'.[10] This would set an unwelcome precedent, as a number of bodies, such as the NCVO, have pointed out. The scandals at the Tate and the Baltic Arts Centre both testify to the hazards of remunerating trustees on the sly, and those bodies which do so officially, such as housing associations, as we have already established, bear even less resemblance to the model of the voluntary and charitable sector that we should be seeking to promote.

Boards of trustees govern the role of an organisation, focusing its objectives and seeking for the best ways to promote them. It is a board of trustees that takes responsibility for preventing mission drift by rejecting proposals for funding and partnership where they run counter to the organisation's objectives or direct it away from its agreed core priorities and values. It is also a board of trustees that is charged with ensuring accountability and transparency.

The fact is that the independence of the sector is virtually enshrined in the fact that voluntary and charitable organisations should be governed by independent, unpaid boards of trustees. Problems arise when a major funder seeks to nominate one or more people to the board, and the NCVO is right to argue that funders should not be entitled to nominate trustees at all.[11] Local authority appointments should be banned. And given the example of such outfits as the Paddington Recreation Ground, it would not be unreasonable to declare that for a body to remain a charity it should not have a statutory body as a trustee. Charities where a statutory body is a trustee should either end that relationship or lose their charitable status.

The Charity Commission

We have already noted how the Charity Commission has failed to assert firmly and strongly a standard of independence which charities should live up to, how it has failed to penalise charities for mission creep, or those whose lobbying and campaigning has become unacceptably political. It should make clear that charities that no longer genuinely operate according to their founders' purposes should seek to rediscover those purposes or shift into another category.

A number of further irregularities are worthy of note. For example, there are on its books, uninvestigated, something in the region of 11,000 dormant charities—that is, charities that that haven't filed an annual report for three or more years. Were they companies, they would have been wiped off the books at Companies House. They could be granted dormant status, or something of the sort, so that those which are genuine could have an opportunity to get up and running again, and those that are simply fronts could sink into desuetude; but despite one policy expert's recommendations to this effect, the Charity Commission has done nothing.

The Charity Commission has come in for a bit of a drubbing when it has been investigated in the past. In examinations carried out in 1988, 1991, 1998, and 2001, the House of Commons Public Accounts Committee was critical of its performance.[12] In the first three of those years it was said to exhibit 'severe shortcomings'.[13] In 1998 it was arraigned for shortcomings in 'management effectiveness, the accuracy of the Register of Charities, the submission of accounts and monitoring of charities, and the support and investigation of charities'.[14] In 2001, despite recognisable improvements, 'the Commission's investigation work' was deemed substandard—'a fact recognised by the Commission itself'.[15]

The Prime Minister's Strategy Unit identified a core tension in 2002, stating that 'the blurring of boundaries between the Commission's advisory and regulatory roles continues to cause confusion among charities and other key stakeholders'.[16] Certain recommendations have already been taken on board in the Charities Act 2006, but challenges remain. The Commission means well, of that there can be little doubt, but it finds itself in a confused position, trying to appear friendly and approachable, and at the same time charged with the responsibility for disciplining those parts of the sector which are not abiding by the rules. It is surely the case that the ambiguous guidance about political lobbying, say, or independence, arises out of its walking such a tricky line.

For the sake of the sector, this needs to be sorted out. It is essential that the Commission distinguishes between the legal and regulatory requirements that charities must comply with, and be firm about them, and the advice and opinion which they may choose to take account of or ignore. It needs to be able to sanction charities that are acting illegally, either through suspension of status or other such measures, and if it is to retain any credibility it needs to make information about charities more openly available for donors, beneficiaries, members and the general public.

None of this is new; it merely needs reasserting. The Strategy Unit has already argued that '[t]he regulator's independence from day-to-day political interference is important and should be preserved',[17] which it is difficult to disagree with, and recommended that the Commission's 'advisory role should be defined in statute to give a clearer focus on regulatory issues'.[18]

Trusts and foundations

With total asset value calculated at £33.3 billion, grant-making charitable trusts and foundations are major funders of the UK voluntary sector, providing about 10 per cent of its income, or £2.7 billion, and they play a critical role in providing general, relatively unrestricted funding to the wide diversity of charitable causes who look to them for support.[19] Although the state's investment in charities dwarfs theirs, they are nevertheless important for safe-guarding the financial—and therefore operational and vocal —independence of voluntary and charitable organisations. The size of their wealth may be less important in policy terms than their power.[20] They are uninhibited by political mandates and the constraints of political legitimacy. They can take on causes that are unpopular or neglected. They can innovate by promoting remedies that are otherwise unfeasible or remote. Although they do not generally perceive themselves as being part of a sector, perhaps the time has come to call on them to act in a collaborative way in order to increase their impact.[21] As Cathy Pharoah has suggested, trusts and foundations could be encouraged to see themselves more actively as guardians of independence.[22]

A comprehensive study of trusts and foundations is beyond the scope of this book,[23] largely because of their range and diversity. There are trusts with a geographical focus, such as some of the Cadbury groups in the West Midlands. There are trusts with restricted objects and policies, such as the Wellcome Trust, which funds only medical research and the history of medicine. There are trusts with a religious basis, such as the Quaker-based Joseph Rowntree Charitable Trust or the Aga Khan Foundation. Trusts can be categorised according to the source of their funds—endowed trusts, personal and family trusts, livery companies, company trusts, public subscription, appeal trusts, and so on. They can be categorised according to the way they give grants—most are gift-givers in that they make grants according to requests, some are investors, some are collaborative entrepreneurs, in that they might set up the bodies to carry out their projects as partners.

Many—though certainly not all—trusts and foundations have traditionally concerned themselves with non-state philanthropy. A large proportion of London's playing fields and parks were acquired by means of grants from the City Parochial Foundation, for example, and Andrew Carnegie, through the Carnegie UK Trust, played a pioneering role in the foundation of public libraries. For the purposes of this study, noteworthy examples—such as the Baring Foundation and the Barrow Cadbury Trust—take a lead by explicitly stating that their interest lies in funding organisations that criticise the status quo. One of the Baring Foundation's three grant-making programmes, for example, is called 'Strengthening the Voluntary Sector'.[24] A great number of others, irrespective of size, tend to concentrate on funding new, recently-discovered or under-recognised needs and problems. They sponsor the promotion of fresh thinking and innovative methods for tackling ongoing and new problems; they focus on disadvantaged and minority groups that have trouble accessing ordinary services, or that are poorly served by them; they look to endorse unpopular work that's hard to finance through conventional fundraising; and they finance work which the government is not yet involved in, or in which it shouldn't be involved.

All the indications are that this independent ethic is very much alive. According to the Association of Charitable Foundations (ACF), which has just over 300 members, accounting for two-thirds of the sector's money,[25] there is a growing reluctance to fund projects or organisations that simply replicate work done by the government:

> We are seeing charities compete for public sector contracts and seeking funds to make up the shortfall... The public perception of charities is changing, particularly when the charity has a large amount of contract income, and trustees are increasingly wary of making grants to these organisations.[26]

This caution is sage and to be encouraged. Trusts and foundations in the twenty-first century might well find they can add most value to the wider voluntary and charitable sector by choosing to fund the kinds of charities which come in under the 30 per cent threshold. The ACF has also observed 'an increase in applications where other types of funding such as SRB (Single Regeneration Budget) had been cut or ended, and for core capital costs, full cost recovery, and running costs'.[27] However, rather than supplement the state they should aim to act outside it. Would trusts and foundations really be adding value by 'subsidising local authorities with charity money'[28] and supporting charities that are already 'raiding their reserves in order to take place in [the contract] market'?[29] The same goes for lottery grants, and trusts should be encouraged to stick to their own priorities, refusing, for example, to provide match funding. It is to their enormous advantage that trusts do not have to conform to agendas or policies, politically correct or otherwise, of government funded bodies such as the Arts Council or Regional Arts Boards.[30]

The best thing about grantmaking trusts is their freedom, and it would be completely wrong to be prescriptive and therefore limit that freedom, but it would certainly be a good thing if they *chose* to use that freedom to safeguard the freedom of other voluntary and charitable organisations. Two further general points can be made about trusts, in terms of their income and in terms of how they spend it. The first is to drive philanthropic giving and the second to support local communities.

Increasing the flow of funds

Trusts and foundations have substantial assets and income, and are able to give large sums of money, but to increase their impact we have to increase the money that is given to them. A good start would be to separate trusts out as a legal entity, so that they are dealt with under trust law. In general, they don't solicit donations from the public or the state to fund their work, but they are regulated in the same way as collecting charities. This has a negative impact. The ACF has voiced its support for 'a regulatory and advisory regime that goes no further than ensuring that grant-making charities make grants within the scope of their objects, that they don't persistently fund poor quality projects, and that their objects reflect the public good'.[31]

The ACF, who are best placed to advise us what trusts and foundations need, have also called for private donations to be kept anonymous. There have been calls for all donations to be publicly declared, but after a struggle the Charities Act 2006 still protects this anonymity. 'A fifth of those who had set up grant-making charities had serious reservations about one or more aspect of doing so,' said the ACF at the end of a three-year investigation into why philanthropists set up foundations, 'the majority of which were related to the burden of bureaucratic regulation.'[32] As for driving money into trusts and foundations from the general public, those that can demonstrate their independence will likely be supported by those who believe in the value of independence.

We find ourselves at an important juncture in the history of philanthropy in this country. Apart from a few names such as Sainsbury, Weston and Rausing, private giving is nowhere near the American league—Buffet giving $31 billion to Bill Gates to add to his $29 billion foundation—but we are nevertheless witnessing a revival. Much of this is owed to the good work being carried out by such bodies as New Philanthropy Capital (NPC), the equivalent of an equity-research firm for the philanthropic marketplace, the Institute of Philanthropy, founded to foster charitable giving in Britain, and Guidestar, which in America has been nicknamed the 'Bloomberg screen of philanthropy',[33] and was launched in this country under the parentage of the Institute of Philanthropy. There are, in addition, a slew of websites—centreforcharityeffectiveness.org; charitygiving.co.uk; charitychoice.co.uk; charityfacts.co.uk; intelligentgiving.com; effectivegiving.com to mention just a few. Added to these, numerous trusts, such as Carnegie UK,[34] are investigating how to promote a culture of giving.

With the stakes high, leverage is important to philanthropists. In 2006 CAF launched two themed charity funds—

the Engaging Young Lives Fund and the Fulfilling Older Lives Fund—which invest in a portfolio of voluntary sector organisations, rather like a unit trust invests in a portfolio of shares. The charities selected for the funds are being audited by NPC. There is some cause for believing that we are witnessing a revolution in what Rockerfeller once called the 'business of beneficence'.

A significant aspect of NPC's mission is to increase the financial injection from the private sector into the voluntary and charitable sector, which plays a significant role in facilitating diversified funding streams for charities. Demanding the kind of efficiency and professionalism that shareholders might expect of the private sector undoubtedly carries risks. For a start, financial efficiency may not actually reflect the extent to which a charity changes lives. It is very difficult, for example, to quantify the good done or value added by the Samaritans. But NPC is alert to these issues, and takes them into account in its evaluations. The key thing to recognise here is that much is being done to promote philanthropic giving in Britain, and trusts and foundations would be wise to collaborate as much as possible with those who are seeking to bring the fruits of capitalism into non-profit-making bodies.

Keeping it local

The way that trusts and foundations go about spending and investing both drives and is driven by the money they can pull in. Driving money into these bodies is not just about impressive feats of philanthropy, but also about the small scale, local and community-based. Just as the majority of third sector organisations are tiny compared with the supercharities, so the majority of the 9,000 or so trusts and foundations are tiny when compared with the big names. While many of these trusts already focus their attentions on local activities, they could be encouraged to do so even more, supporting local charities and community associations, and even setting up or sponsoring community trusts formed to act as a focus for local giving by companies and individuals. Public giving is closely related to a sense of ownership. If trusts and foundations, as well as charities, can demonstrate that they belong in civil society, and are not the instruments of government, then public giving is likely to be resurgent.

Engaging citizens as active participants in their communities would almost certainly bring about an increase in public giving, if not volunteering. Much of the fall in volunteering, much of people's disengagement from their neighbourhoods, is not the consequence of government or charity policy, but the result of busier lifestyles, consumerism, and social atomisation; but that does not mean there is nothing that voluntary and charitable bodies can do to reverse the trend. Community Foundations already exist, situated in 48 local areas, and these offer some kind of a model, although they are closely bound in with statutory authorities.[35] Some are major grantmakers. They mainly fundraise locally and build their endowments from local community donations. They offer sustainable local funding for local needs. The total assets of the Community Foundation Network members have grown by nearly 30 per cent in the last year.[36] This is the kind of thing that existing trusts and foundations could look to be involved in as they seek to endow and encourage the communities that will in turn support them—and as we seek to build a voluntary and charitable sector that is truly independent.

Putting a fence round animal farm

This book hardly scratches the surface of what can be said about the sector, and researching it, and meeting a wide range of expert and experienced people, has been an engaging and often humbling experience. There is so much more to say. Those well acquainted with the field will have been quick to notice that I have not touched on charities that have become more a part of the private sector—community businesses, social enterprises and the like—but I do not think that yet poses a threat equal to that of the state's incursion. Vast reams of research are available for the interested reader, research by people with a passion for the spirit of community and associative democracy, research by people who are thinking about how to make Britain a better place. There are bound to be those who disagree with the suggestions contained in this chapter. But dispute and debate are better than compliant silence.

Alexis de Tocqueville said that a democratically elected government works for the happiness of the citizenry, but wants to be the only agent and final arbiter of that happiness. He concluded that '[a]mong democratic nations it is only by association that the resistance of the people to the government can ever display itself: hence the latter always looks with ill favour on those associations which are not in its power'.[37] Fittingly, Hilary Armstrong, Minister for the Cabinet Office and Social Exclusion and Chancellor of the Duchy of Lancaster, has scornfully said that those who express unease about the growing trend for state intervention in the third sector are 'whingeing',[38] just as Stephen Bubb, the chief executive of ACEVO, which pushes for greater integration of charity into the state, has also spoken dismissively of the sector's 'whinge-fest'.[39]

Hopefully, however, the case has been made that there *are* reasonable grounds for questioning the nature of the relationship as it stands between the voluntary and charitable sector and the state. It is my belief that we should be proud of where we've come from as a nation, concerned about where we are, and optimistic about where we could be going. But change is necessary to fuel that optimism. The line of this book has not been to condemn state support of the third sector, but rather to express reservations about the terms of that support and to seek to promote and encourage those organisations wishing to remain independent of that support. In order to achieve this, we need to accept that, while there are some things the state can do better than any other sector, and while it should carry on doing these, the blurring of the divisions between the sectors is proving detrimental to a large number of voluntary and charitable organisations—and the civil society to which they belong.

For the third sector can do what it does better than the state ever could, and better than it can when morphed into a clone of the state. The distinctive value of the third sector lies in its ability to think about and respond to the needs of our society in a way that government cannot. Giving to voluntary and charitable organisations provides each of us as individuals with the chance to become active players in bringing about the changes we want to see in the world. So if animal farm syndrome describes the growing resemblance of parts of the voluntary and charitable sector to the state, then we are going to need more securely to fence the farm. Organisations would then be presented with a starker choice as to where they want to position themselves. We have to seek to limit the spread of this syndrome before the entire sector starts to look like it's been nationalised.

If the parastatal agencies are here to stay, and the bureaucracies of compassion are here to stay, and the powerful lobbying and campaigning organisations are here to stay, then we're going to have to make sure that in sustaining them we do not do away with the many small, expert, local organisations that don't seek to influence public policy or the legislative process, but which have played and play such a vital role in building this liberal democracy of which we should be so proud. We want inclusive communities. We want diversity and individuality. We want fire in the belly. The time for change has come.

Abbreviations

Most of the abbreviations used in this book will be familiar to the general reader, but a few pop up here and there that could cause confusion to anyone not involved in the voluntary and charitable sector, and these are set out below for reference.

Abbreviation

ACEVO	Association of Chief Executives of Voluntary Organisations
ACF	Association of Charitable Foundations
CAF	Charities Aid Foundation
NCVO	National Council for Voluntary Organisations
NGO	Non-governmental organisation
NPC	New Philanthropy Capital
SRB	Single Regeneration Budget
SORP	Statement of Recommended Practice

Notes

Foreword

1   The Elizabethan statute was not repealed until 1888, 'and even then the new statute carefully preserved the preamble and its list of uses properly regarded as charitable... the precise word "charitable" has acquired a meaning that is anchored in the language of the preamble.' Jordan, W.K., *Philanthropy in England 1480-1660: A Study of the Changing Patterns of English Social Aspirations*, London: George Allen and Unwin, 1959, p. 113.

2   Lord Macnaghten, *The Commissioners of Income Tax v. Pemsel*, A.C.521. Quoted in Owen, D., *English Philanthropy 1660-1960*, Cambridge Ma: Harvard University Press, 1965, p. 324.

3   Knowles, D., *Bare Ruined Choirs: The Dissolution of the English Monasteries*, Cambridge: Cambridge University Press, 1976, chapter 5.

Introduction

1   Dahrendorf, R., 'Foreword', *Dimensions of the Voluntary Sector*, London: CAF, 1997, pp. 7-8.

2   Gladstone, F.J., *Voluntary Action in a Changing World*, London: Bedford Square Press, 1979, pp. 3-4.

3   Charity Commission, 'Policy Statement on Charities and Public Service Delivery', June 2005.

4   *Public Action, Private Benefit: A Review of Charities and the Wider Not-For-Profit Sector*, London: Cabinet Office, 2002, p. 7.

5   *The Times*, 3 May 1988, cited by Frank Prochaska in a speech delivered at the UCL, 'Is Voluntary Action in Decline?', 29 June 2006, pp. 3-4.

6   Quoted in Griffith, M., Jochum, V. and Wilding, K., *Voluntary Sector Strategic Analysis 2006/07*, London: NCVO, 2006, p. 27.

7   Hanvey, C. and Philpot, T. (eds), *Sweet Charity: The Role and Workings of Voluntary Organisations*, London: Routledge, 1996, p. 11.

8   Blackmore, A., *Standing Apart, Working Together: a study of the myths and realities of voluntary and community sector independence*, London: NCVO, 2004, pp. 35, 40.

9   *UK Voluntary Sector Almanac 2006*, London: NCVO, 2006.

10   Kendall, J., *The Voluntary Sector: Comparative Perspectives in the UK*, London: Routledge, 2003, p. 25.

11   Charity Commission, RR7: 'The independence of Charities from the State', 2001.

12   'The future of public services: a briefing and discussion paper', London: NCVO, 2003, para. 5.5.

13   Harker, A. and Burkeman, S., *Stepping Up the Stairs: Increasing the Impact of Progressive Philanthropy in the UK*, London: Carnegie United Kingdom Trust, 2005, p. 7.

14   Blake, G., Robinson, D. and Smerdon, M., *Living Values: A Report Encouraging Boldness in Third Sector Organisations*, London: Community Links, 2006, p. 11.

1: What is Charity?

1   Gutch, R., Kunz, C. and Spencer, K., *Partners or Agents?* London: NCVO, 1990, p. 6. Cited by Jones, R., 'Swimming together: statutory and voluntary', in Hanvey, C. and Philpot, T. (eds), *Sweet Charity: The Role and Workings of Voluntary Organisations*, London: Routledge, 1996, p. 43.

2   http://www.charity-commission.gov.uk/registeredcharities/factfigures.asp

3   *Public Action, Private Benefit: A Review of Charities and the Wider Not-For-Profit Sector*, London: Cabinet Office, 2002, p. 19.

4   Pharoah, C., Walker, W., Goodey, L. and Clegg, S., *Charity Trends 2006*, London: CAF, 2006 p. 36.

5   Charity Commission press release, 'What makes people trust charity?', 4 November 2005.

6   Guidestar: http://search.guidestar.org.uk/cgi-bin/search?v per
    cent3afile=viv_tClmI5&v:state=root per cent7Croot-40-20 per
    cent7C0

7   *Public Action, Private Benefit*, 2002, p. 14.

8   *Public Action, Private Benefit*, 2002, p. 15.

9   Salamon, L. and Anheier, H., *Defining the Nonprofit Sector: A Cross
    National Analysis*, Manchester: Manchester University Press, 1997,
    pp. 29-34.

10 Kendall, J., and Knapp, M., *The Voluntary Sector in the UK*,
    Manchester: Manchester University Press, 1996, p. 111.

11 *UK Voluntary Sector Almanac 2006*, London: NCVO, 2006.

12 http://www.cafonline.org/research/factsandfigures.cfm

13 Morris, S., 'Defining the Nonprofit Sector: Some Lessons from
    History', *Voluntas*, vol. 11, no. 1, 2000, pp. 25-44.

14 Kendall J. and Knapp, M., *The Voluntary Sector in the UK*,
    Manchester: Manchester University Press, 1996, p. 20.

15 Joint Committee on Draft Bill, p. 19. Cited in Smith, R. and
    Whittington, P., *Charity: The Spectre of Over-regulation and State
    Dependency*, London: CPS, 2006, unpublished draft, p. 36.

16 Picarda, H., *The Law and Practice Relating to Charities*, 3rd edition,
    London: Butterworths, 1999, p. 1. See also: Chesterman, M.,
    Charities, Trusts and Social Welfare, London: Weidenfeld and
    Nicolson, 1979, Part 1.

17 Picarda, *The Law and Practice Relating to Charities*, 1999, p. 1. See
    also: Chesterman, *Charities, Trusts and Social Welfare*, 1979, Part 1.

18 Joint Committee on Draft Bill, p. 19, para. 63. Smith and
    Whittington, *Charity*, CPS, 2006, unpublished draft, p. 36.

19 Charity Commission, 'Public Benefit - the legal principles', para 2,
    January 2005, http://www.charity-commission.gov.uk/spr/pblp.asp

2: How Have We Got Here?

[1] Blackmore, A., *Standing Apart, Working Together:: A Study of the Myths and Realities of Voluntary and Community Sector Independence*, London: NCVO, 2004, p. 10.

[2] Griffith, M., Jochum, V. and Wilding, K., *Voluntary Sector Strategic Analysis 2006/07*, London: NCVO, 2006, p. 27. (Though the Home Office has for some time had a third sector division, until recently the Active Communities Directorate.)

[3] Owen, D., *English Philanthropy 1660-1960*, Cambridge, Mass: Harvard University Press, 1965, *passim*.

[4] Jordan, W.K., *Philanthropy in England: 1480-1660: A Study of the Changing Pattern of English Social Aspirations*, London: George Allen and Unwin, 1959.

[5] Picarda, *The Law and Practice Relating to Charities*, 1999, p 1. See also: Chesterman, *Charities, Trusts and Social Welfare*, 1979, Part 1; and Jordan, *Philanthropy in England: 1480-1660*, 1959, pp. 112-13.

[6] Stone, L., *History*, XLIV, 1959, pp. 257-60; Coleman, D.C., *Economic History Review*, 2nd series XIII, 1960, pp. 113-15; Bittle, W.G. and Lane, R.T., 'Inflation and Philanthropy in England: A Re-assessment of W.K. Jordan's Data', *Economic History Review*, 2nd series XXIX, 1976, pp. 203-10.

[7] Jordan, *Philanthropy in England: 1480-1660*, 1959, p. 119.

[8] Jones, M.G., *The Charity School Movement*, Cambridge: Cambridge University Press, 1938, p. 38. Cited in Owen, *English Philanthropy 1660-1960*, 1965, p. 24.

[9] Owen, *English Philanthropy 1660-1960*, 1965, pp. 30-31.

[10] Pharoah, C., Walker, W., Goodey, L. and Clegg, S., *Charity Trends 2006*, London: CAF, 2006 p. 37, adding together cancer, chest & heart, health advocacy/information/research, hospices, hospitals and HIV/Aids. Also *UK Voluntary Sector Almanac 2006*, London: NCVO, 2006, p. 4: 'Medical research attracts more donors than any other cause… The other most popular causes were hospitals and hospices and young people's causes'.

[11] Stephen, J., *Essays in Ecclesiastical Biography*, 2 vols., London: Longman, 1849, i, p. 382, quoted in Prochaska, F., *The Voluntary Impulse: Philanthropy in Modern Britain*, London: Faber and Faber, 1988, pp. 39-40.

[12] Lewis, J., *The Voluntary Sector, the State and Social Work in Britain*, Aldershot: Edward Elgar, 1995, p. 5.

[13] See Prochaska, F.K., 'Philanthropy', in Thompson, F.M.L. (ed.), *The Cambridge Social History of Britain 1750-1950*, vol. 3, Cambridge: Cambridge University Press, 1990, p. 358.

[14] *The Times*, 9 January 1885, cited in Owen, *English Philanthropy 1660-1960*, 1965, p. 469.

[15] Prochaska, 'Philanthropy', in Thompson, *The Cambridge Social History of Britain 1750-1950*, vol. 3, 1990, p. 384 & 358.

[16] Harris, J., 'Society and State in Twentieth-Century Britain', in Thompson, F.M.L. (ed.), *The Cambridge Social History of Britain 1750-1950*, vol. 3, *Social Agencies and Institutions*, Cambridge: Cambridge University Press, 1990. Cited in Lewis, *The Voluntary Sector*, 1995, p. 1.

[17] Owen, *English Philanthropy 1660-1960*, 1965, p. 95.

[18] Lewis, *The Voluntary Sector*, 1995, p. 6.

[19] Bradley, I.C., *Enlightened Entrepreneurs*, London: Weidenfeld and Nicolson, 1987, *passim*.

[20] Prahms, W., *Newcastle Ragged and Industrial School*, Stroud: Tempus, 2006, p. 13.

[21] Heasman, K., *Evangelicals in Action: An Appraisal of their Social Work in the Victorian Era*, London: Geoffrey Bles, 1962, p. 11.

[22] de Tocqueville, A., *Democracy in America*, Modern Library edn, New York, 1981, pp. 556, 578. See also Larry Siedentop, *Tocqueville*, Oxford: Oxford University Press, 1994, pp. 92-95.

[23] de Tocqueville, A., *Democracy in America*, Book II, Ch. 5.

[24] Mill, J.S., *Principles of Political Economy*, Harmondsworth: Penguin, 1970, pp. 312-13.

25 Urwick, E.J., *A Philosophy of Social Progress*, London: Methuen, 1912, p. 194. Cited in Lewis, *The Voluntary Sector*, 1995, p. 7.

26 Lewis, *The Voluntary Sector*, 1995, p. 75.

27 Harris, 'Society and the State in Twentieth-Century Britain', in Thompson, *The Cambridge Social History of Britain 1750-1950*, vol. 3. *Social Agencies and Institutions*, 1990, p. 67.

28 Harris, 'Society and the State in Twentieth-Century Britain', in Thompson, *The Cambridge Social History of Britain 1750-1950*, vol. 3. *Social Agencies and Institutions*, 1990, p. 67.

29 Thane, P., 'Government and Society in England and Wales, 1750-1914', in Thompson, *The Cambridge Social History of Britain 1750-1950*, vol. 3. *Social Agencies and Institutions*, 1990, p. 1.

30 *Labour Leader*, 29 September 1905. Cited in Wagner, G., *Barnardo*, London: Weidenfeld and Nicholson, 1979, p. 299.

31 Gray, B.K., *Philanthropy and the State, or Social Politics*, London: P.S. King, 1908, p. 154.

32 Holland, H.S., *A Bundle of Memories*, 1915, pp. 280-81.

33 The consequences of the decision by Parliament to pay for indiscriminate admissions to the Foundling Hospital in the 1750s are described in McClure, R.K., *Coram's Children: The London Foundling Hospital in the Eighteenth Century*, London: Yale University Press, 1981, pp. 76-136. The history of the RNLI's brief dependence on public subsidy is told in Warner, O., *The Life-Boat Service*, London, 1974, p. 37 ff.

34 West, E.G., *Education and the State*, London: Institute of Economic Affairs, 2nd edn 1970 (1965), pp. xxvii & 132.

35 West, *Education and the State*, 2nd edn 1970, p. 137ff. The National Society described itself as 'constrained by a deep sense of the inconvenience which would arise from admitting into the National Schools an official inspection not derived from or connected with the Authorities of the National Church.' Quoted in Gray, *Philanthropy and the State, or Social Politics*, 1908, p. 140.

36 Prahms, *Newcastle Ragged and Industrial School*, 2006, p. 9.

37 The 1854 Young Offenders Act, 1866 Reformatory Schools Act and 1857, 1861 and 1866 Industrial Schools Acts.

38 Prahms, *Newcastle Ragged and Industrial School*, 2006, p. 12.

39 Prahms, *Newcastle Ragged and Industrial School*, 2006, pp. 9 and 11.

40 Prahms, *Newcastle Ragged and Industrial School*, 2006, p. 15.

41 *The Times*, January 1873, cited in Prahms, *Newcastle Ragged and Industrial School*, 2006, p. 16. See also Dennis, N., *The Uncertain Trumpet: a History of Church of England School Education to AD 2001*, London: Civitas, 2001, pp. 1-10.

42 Whelan, R., (ed.), *Octavia Hill's Letter's to Fellow-Workers 1872-1911*, London: Kyrle, 2005, p. 39.

43 Quoted in Pollock, J., *Shaftesbury: The Poor Man's Earl*, London: Hodder and Stoughton, 1985, p. 152.

44 For a full account of this, see West, *Education and the State*, 2nd edn, 1970, pp. 157-59.

45 Heasman, *Evangelicals in Action*, 1962, pp. 66-7, 243-45.

46 Gray, *Philanthropy and the State, or Social Politics*, 1908, p. 297.

47 Braithwaite, C., *The Voluntary Citizen: an Enquiry into the Place of Philanthropy in the Community*, London: Methuen, 1938, p. 16.

48 Beveridge, W., *Voluntary Action*, London, 1948, p. 318.

49 Beveridge, *Voluntary Action*, 1948, p. 320.

50 See Owen, *English Philanthropy 1660-1960*, 1965, p. 573. An extreme example of this was the Royal Surgical Aids Society, which found itself almost completely redundant in a National Health Service, but with invested funds amounting to £250,000. Under the scope of *cy-près* legislation, the trustees were permitted by the court to use the funds to establish homes for the elderly.

51 See Hanvey, C. and Philpot, T. (eds), *Sweet Charity: The Role and Workings of Voluntary Organisations*, London: Routledge, 1996, p. 1. 'We hold two conflicting views of charity. In the first it is perceived as "cold", uncaring and covered in the barnacles of nineteenth-century workhouses, watery gruel and mean-spirited care. The

second recognises this as a largely outmoded view, arguing that, despite a chequered past, a vibrant voluntary sector is a complementary part of any welfare state.'

52 There is a good discussion of this in Prochaska, F., *Christianity and Social Service in Modern Britain*, Oxford: Oxford University Press, 2006, pp. 162-64.

53 Lewis, *The Voluntary Sector*, 1995, p. 20.

54 Malpass, P., 'The Restructuring of Social Rented Housing in Britain: Demunicipalization and the Rise of Registered Social Landlords', *European Journal of Housing Policy*, 1 (1), 2001, 8-12.

55 Jenkins, S., 'The welfare state is waning. Bring on the philanthropists', *Guardian*, 28 June 2006.

56 Lewis, *The Voluntary Sector*, 1995, p. 20.

57 Rochester, C., *A Handbook for Small Voluntary Agencies: Building the Capacity of Small Voluntary Agencies*, London: LSE, repr. 2000, pp. 2-8.

58 Leigh, G., 'Public opinion', *The Times*, 11 June 2006.

59 *The Times*, 17 December, 1984.

60 NCVO, *Voluntary Sector Almanac 2004*.

61 *UK Voluntary Sector Almanac 2006*.

62 See Pharoah, Walker, Goodey and Clegg, *Charity Trends 2006*, 2006, p. 26. The figure is 45 per cent until we add—which we will argue we should—Lottery and Arts Council funding, which accounts for a further two per cent. CAF shares its data collection methods and parameters with the NCVO, so these figures are comparable.

63 Kendall, *The Voluntary Sector: Comparative Perspectives in the UK*, 2003, p. 25.

64 Prochaska, F., *The Voluntary Impulse: Philanthropy in Modern Britain*, London: Faber and Faber, 1988, p. 4.

65 Frank Prochaska, 'Is Voluntary Action in Decline?' speech delivered at the UCL, 29 June 2006, p. 9. For a discussion of state sponsored voluntarism, see Hirst, P., *Associative Democracy: New*

Forms for Economic and Social Governance, Cambridge: Cambridge University Press, 1994, chapter 6.

3: The Golden Rule

1   Dahrendorf, R., *House of Lords Hansard*, 20 January 2005, Column 938.

2   Interview with Sam Brier, ex-chief executive of charity KIDS.

3   The organisation's full title is: Catholic Children's Society (Arundel & Brighton, Portsmouth and Southwark). Quoted in Philpot, T., 'Paying the price for filling the coffers', *The Tablet*, 18 February 2006.

4   Telephone interview with Clare McKeown, head of international donor development, Save the Children, 11 May 2006.

5   Blackmore, A., *Standing Apart, Working Together: A Study of the Myths and Realities of Voluntary and Community Sector Independence*, London: NCVO, 2004, p. 31.

6   Letter, Chris Hanvey, UK Director of Operations, Barnardo's, 10 October 2006.

7   Blackmore, *Standing Apart, Working Together*, 2004, p. 31.

8   Quoted in Philpot, 'Paying the price for filling the coffers', *The Tablet*, 18 February 2006.

9   Leonard Cheshire, 'Why voluntary income is essential', http://www.leonard-cheshire.org/?lid=15

10 NCVO, *Working Party Report on Effectiveness and the Voluntary Sector*, London: NCVO, 1990, para. 2.12.

11 See *Compact: Working Together Better Together*, www.thecompact.org.uk

12 See Deakin, N., 'Voluntary Inaction', in Whelan, R. (ed.), *Involuntary Action*, London: Institute of Economic Affairs, 1999, pp. 27-34.

13 Chapman, R., 'Are charities the new public sector?', *Guardian*, 21 March 2006.

[14] Interview with Nigel Haynes, director of Fairbridge, 3 July 2006.

[15] NCVO research, cited in Kelly, A., 'Promises, promises', *Guardian*, 28 June 2006.

[16] Chapman, R., 'Are charities the new public sector?' *Guardian*, 21 March 2006.

[17] A comprehensive discussion of the issues surrounding full cost recovery and other intricacies of the contracting process can be found in Blackmore, A., Bush H. and Bhutta, M., *The Reform of Public Services: the Role of the Voluntary Sector*, London: NCVO, Annex A, 2005.

[18] Blake, G., Robinson, D. and Smerdon, M., *Living Values: A Report Encouraging Boldness in Third Sector Organisations*, London: Community Links, 2006, p. 26.

[19] Brookes, M. and Copps, J., *Surer Funding: Improving Third Sector Public Service Delivery*, London: Association of Chief Executives of Voluntary Organisations, 2005.

[20] *Home Office: Working with the Third Sector*, London: National Audit Office, 2005, p. 4.

[21] Brookes, M. and Copps, J., 'A Surer Funding Framework for Improved Public Services', London: New Philanthropy Capital, 2005, pp. 1-2.

[22] Harris, M., 'Voluntary Organisations in a Changing Social Policy Environment', in Harris, M. and Rochester, C. (eds), *Voluntary Organisations and Social Policy in Britain: Perspectives on Change and Choice*, Houndmills: Palgrave, 2001, p. 220.

[23] Telephone interview with Joyce Moseley, Chief Executive of Rainer, 3 May 2006; telephone interview with Dr Chris Hanvey, UK Director of Operations, Barnardo's, 22 May 2006.

[24] This example is taken from Brookes and Copps, *Surer Funding: Improving Third Sector Public Service Delivery*, 2005.

[25] Brookes and Copps, *Surer Funding: Improving Third Sector Public Service Delivery*, 2005.

[26] *Home Office: Working with the Third Sector*, 2005, p. 4.

27 Leigh, G., 'Public opinion', *The Times*, 11 July 2006.

28 This case study is taken from a speech delivered by Iain Duncan Smith MP at '*Third Sector* magazine, Britain's Most Admired Charities Awards', 3 November 2005.

29 The organisation's full name is: Catholic Children's Society (Arundel & Brighton, Portsmouth and Southwark). Quoted in Philpot, 'Paying the price for filling the coffers', *The Tablet*, 18 February 2006.

30 Philpot, T., *NCH Action for Children: The Story of Britain's Foremost Children's Charity*, Oxford: Lion, 1994, p. 108.

31 This example is taken from West, T., 'Hung out to dry', *New Start*, 30 November 2001.

32 West, 'Hung out to dry', *New Start*, 30 November 2001.

33 A sample of 1,036 charities has been examined, but the findings were inconclusive.

34 http://www.europa.eu/scadplus/leg/en/lvb/e50017.htm. See also: NICVA's response to the Draft National Strategic Reference Document, May 2006, p. 1.

35 Griffith, M., Jochum, V. and Wilding, K., *Voluntary Sector Strategic Analysis 2006/07*, London: NCVO, 2006, p. 28.

36 'Changing funding programmes: impact on the work of the voluntary and community sector and consequences for the Yorkshire and Humber economy'. Cited in Griffith, Jochum and Wilding, *Voluntary Sector Strategic Analysis 2006/07*, 2006, p. 28.

37 Blake, Robinson and Smerdon, *Living Values*, 2006, p. 26.

38 Interview with Nigel Haynes, director of Fairbridge, 3 July 2006.

39 Blackmore, Bush and Bhutta, *The Reform of Public Services: The Role of the Voluntary Sector*, p. 34.

40 *Home Office: Working with the Third Sector*, 2005, pp. 45-48.

41 Interview with Nigel Haynes, director of Fairbridge, 3 July 2006.

42 Interview with Stuart Etherinton, director of NCVO, 2 July 2006.

[43] Gaskin, K., *Reasonable Care? Risk, Risk Management and Volunteering in England*, London: Volunteering England, 2005, cited in Griffith, Jochum and Wilding, *Voluntary Sector Strategic Analysis 2006/07*, 2006, p. 21. See also: Wynne-Jones, J., 'Cleaning a church is "just too risky" for teen volunteers', *Sunday Telegraph*, 16 July 2006.

[44] See Rochester, C., 'Regulation: The Impact on Local Voluntary Action,' in Harris and Rochester, *Voluntary Organisations and Social Policy in Britain*, 2001, pp. 64-80.

[45] Taylor, M., 'Partnership: Insiders and Outsiders,' in Harris and Rochester, *Voluntary Organisations and Social Policy in Britain*, 2001, p. 98.

[46] Telephone interview with Joyce Moseley, chief executive of Rainer, 3 May 2006.

[47] Gibben, C., Robb, C. and Wilding, K., *The Third Sector: Vision for the Future*, London: NCVO, 2002, pp. 21-22.

[48] Deakin, N., speech delivered at the LSE conference, 'An Independent Sector?', 7 April 2003. Cited in Blackmore, *Standing Apart, Working Together*, 2004, p. 20.

[49] Interview with David Emerson, director of the Association of Charitable Foundations, 5 May 2006.

[50] Interview with Nigel Haynes, director of Fairbridge, 3 July 2006.

[51] The trustee of one such charity said that when a charity has a very low profile 'it is even more difficult to fund raise from corporate givers and also from the public'. So they are forced, in order to sustain their services, to draw from the Treasury's coffers.

[52] Interview with Dr Chris Hanvey, UK director of operations, Barnardo's, 19 April 2006.

[53] Interview with Darlene Corry, head of policy, Women's Resource Centre, 7 August 2006.

[54] Cited in Blake, Robinson and Smerdon, *Living Values*, 2006, p. 11.

[55] Blackmore, *Standing Apart, Working Together*, 2004, p. 19.

[56] 'The Efficiency Scrutiny of government funding of the sector carried out by the Home Office in 1990... laid down the principle that clear benefit for official policies must result from such funding... "*Departments... should establish clear policy objectives for any core or project grant or scheme, relating to objectives in departments' planning processes. Grants or schemes which no longer relate to such objectives should be phased out*"'. *Meeting the Challenge of Change: Voluntary Action into the 21st Century, The Report of the Commission on the Future of the Voluntary Sector*, London: NCVO, 1996, pp. 3, 45.

[57] Charity Commission, 'Policy Statement on Charities and Public Service Delivery', June 2005.

[58] Cited in Blake, Robinson and Smerdon, *Living Values*, 2006, p. 28.

[59] Cited in Blake, Robinson and Smerdon, *Living Values*, 2006, p. 28.

[60] Flynn, N., 'A mixed blessing? How the contract culture works', in Hanvey, C. and Philpot, T. (eds), *Sweet Charity: The Role and Workings of Voluntary Organisations*, London: Routledge, 1996, p. 61.

[61] Flynn, 'A mixed blessing?', in Hanvey and Philpot, *Sweet Charity*, 1996, p. 62.

[62] Blackmore, *Standing Apart, Working Together*, 2004, p. 29.

[63] Shaw, G. Bernard, *Pygmalion*, (1914) Harmondsworth: Penguin Books, 1965, p.59.

[64] Rooff, M., *A Hundred Years of Family Welfare: A study of the Family Welfare Association (Charity Organisation Society) 1869-1969*, London: Michael Joseph, 1972, p. 321.

[65] Whelan, R., *Helping the Poor: Friendly Visiting, Dole Charities and Dole Queues*, London: Civitas, 2001, appendix 2.

[66] Pinker, R., 'Social work and social policy in the twentieth century: retrospect and prospect', in Bulmer, M. *et al.* (eds), *The Goals of Social Policy*, London: Unwin Hyman, 1989, p. 86.

[67] Pringle, J., 'COS Annual Reports 1933-37', quoted in Rooff, *A Hundred Years of Family Welfare*, 1972, p. 131.

[68] Rooff, *A Hundred Years of Family Welfare*, 1972, p. 228.

[69] Ironically, as Madeline Rooff was finishing her book, the FWA was experiencing a financial crisis that resulted in the creation of a Board of Management to take responsibility for all of the organisation's affairs. *A Hundred Years of Family Welfare*, 1972, p. 232.

[70] Lewis, J., *The Voluntary Sector, the State and Social Work in Britain*, Aldershot: Edward Elgar, 1995, p. 124. The remaining part of this case study is drawn from Lewis's excellent survey of the sector through the lens of the FWA.

[71] Lewis, *The Voluntary Sector*, 1995, p. 145.

[72] Lewis, *The Voluntary Sector*, 1995, pp. 142-45.

[73] Lewis, *The Voluntary Sector*, 1995, pp. 148-59.

[74] *Home Office: Working with the Third Sector*, 2005, p. 2.

[75] COS, *52nd Annual Report for 1919-20*, London: COS, 1920. Cited in Lewis, *The Voluntary Sector*, 1995, p. 85.

[76] Lewis, *The Voluntary Sector*, 1995, pp. 1, 17-19.

[77] Flanders, T., 'The Samaritan and Caesar', *Religion and Liberty*, vol. 9, no. 3, Acton Institute, 1999, p. 2.

[78] Quoted in Tanner, M., *The Poverty of Welfare: Helping Other in Civil Society*, Washington: Cato, 2003, p. 121.

[79] Tanner, *The Poverty of Welfare*, 2003, p. 121.

[80] Tanner, *The Poverty of Welfare*, 2003, p. 123.

[81] Email from Matthew Wilson, director, The Message Trust, 9 May 2006.

[82] From 'The Dwellings of the Poor', 1883, quoted in Goodwin, M. (ed.), *Nineteenth Century Opinion: An Anthology of Extracts from 'The Nineteenth Century'*, 1877-1901, Harmondsworth: Penguin, 1951, p. 75.

[83] The Shaftesbury Society Report and Financial Statements for year ended 31 March 2005, p. 4.

84 The Shaftesbury Society Report and Financial Statements for year ended 31 March 2005, p. 16.

85 Philpot, *NCH Action for Children*, 1994, p. 64.

86 Special meeting of the Council, 20 March 1946, quoted in Rose, J., *For the Sake of the Children: Inside Dr Barnardo's, 120 Years of Caring for Children*, London: Hodder and Stoughton, 1987, p. 206.

87 Special meeting of the Council, 20 March 1946, quoted in Rose, *For the Sake of the Children*, 1987, p. 202.

88 Nathan Report, Q. 6850, quoted in Owen, D., *English Philanthropy 1660-1960*, Cambridge, Mass: Harvard University Press, 1965, p. 543.

89 Litten, J., *Blueprints: The Reconstruction Plans of the National Children's Home*, National Children's Home, 1943, quoted in Philpot, *NCH Action for Children*, 1994, p. 83.

90 Philpot, *NCH Action for Children*, 1994, pp. 174-77.

91 Prochaska, F., *Christianity and Social Service in Modern Britain*, Oxford: Oxford University Press, 2006, p. 171.

92 *The Future of Voluntary Organisations: Report on the Wolfenden Committee*, London: Croom-Helm, 1978, p. 185.

93 *Barnardo's Then and Now*, Barnardo's, 2005.

94 Interview with Sarah Roberts, head of fundraising at Rainbow Trust, 11 April 2006: 'Government funding would restrict the flexibility of the care provision that we can offer... at present we do not fit the funding requirements and we are not going to change our policies so that we do.' Interview with David Howarth, chief executive of Honeypot, 13 June 2006. 'I guess we don't take government money because we traditionally haven't. We're alert to the dangers of relying heavily on government money... we're conscious of the dangers of permitting government contracts to dictate our policy.'

95 Thomas, N., 'New frontiers: Angela Greatley, chief executive, Sainsbury Centre for Mental Health', *Third Sector*, 19 April 2006.

[96] Thomas, 'New frontiers: Angela Greatley, chief executive, Sainsbury Centre for Mental Health', *Third Sector*, 19 April 2006.

4: Politicising Charity

[1] HMRC Budget 2006, A.117.

[2] Pharoah, C., Walker, W., Goodey, L. and Clegg, S., *Charity Trends 2006*, London: CAF, 2006, p. 28.

[3] Flynn, N., 'A mixed blessing? How the contract culture works', in Hanvey, C. and Philpot, T. (eds), *Sweet Charity: The Role and Workings of Voluntary Organisations*, London: Routledge, 1996, p. 63.

[4] Hayes, V., letter, 'Pushed out', *Guardian*, 15 November 2006.

[5] Interview with Dr Chris Hanvey, 19 April 2006.

[6] Richardson, J., *Purchase of Service Contracting: Some Evidence on UK Implementation*, London: NCVO, 1995, p. 13.

[7] Telephone interview with David Emerson, director, Association of Charitable Foundations, 5 May 2006.

[8] Interview with Bernard Gesch, director Natural Justice, 6 June 2006. Email, 1 November 2006: 'To demonstrate cause requires rigorous double blind experimental studies and these have not been done... and according to a US report "the most commonly used non-randomized study designs often produce erroneous conclusions and can lead to practices that are ineffective or harmful"'. See also Felicity Lawrence, 'Delayed: the food study that could cut prison violence by 'up to 40%', *Guardian*, 17 October 2006.

[9] See also: Martin, N., *Marriage on MARS: How the government's MARS programme provides resources to organisations that do not support marriage*, London: Civitas, 2003.

[10] See for instance Tanner, M., *The Poverty of Welfare: Helping Other in Civil Society*, Washington: Cato, 2003, p. 102.

[11] Turning Point Annual Report, 2005.

[12] Iain Duncan Smith MP at 'Third Sector magazine, Britain's Most Admired Charities Awards', 3 November 2005.

[13] Iain Duncan Smith MP at 'Third Sector magazine, Britain's Most Admired Charities Awards', 3 November 2005.

[14] Chapman, R., 'Are charities the new public sector?', Guardian, 21 March 2006.

[15] Telephone interview with Clare McKeown, head of international donor development, Save the Children, 11 May 2006.

[16] Blackmore, A., Standing Apart, Working Together: A Study of the Myths and Realities of Voluntary and Community Sector Independence, London: NCVO, 2004, p. 27.

[17] Blake, G., Robinson, D. and Smerdon, M., Living Values: A Report Encouraging Boldness in Third Sector Organisations, London: Community Links, 2006, p. 26.

[18] Joy, I., and Miller, I., Don't Mind Me: Adults with Mental Health Problems, London: NPC, 2006, p. 66.

[19] Interview with Maurice Wren, director Asylum Aid, 7 August 2006.

[20] Speaking Truth to Power: A Discussion Paper on the Voluntary Sector's Relationship with Government, London: Baring Foundation, 2000, p. 6.

[21] Gibben, C., Robb, C. and Wilding, K., The Third Sector: Vision for the Future, London: NCVO, 2002. Cited in Blackmore, Standing Apart, Working Together, 2004, p. 28.

[22] Prochaska, F., 'Is Voluntary Action in Decline?', speech delivered at the UCL, 29 June 2006, p. 9.

[23] Blackmore, Standing Apart, Working Together, 2004, p. 29.

[24] Blackmore, Standing Apart, Working Together, 2004, p. 29.

[25] See, for instance, Office of the Children's Rights Commissioner for London, Changing Schools: the Impact of the Schools Admission Process on Children, 2002. The address at the bottom—94 White Lion Street, London—is the same as the CRAE.

26   CRAE Member organisations:
http://www.crae.org.uk/cms/index.php?option=com_content&task
=view&id=25&Itemid=61.

27   Telephone interview, Louise King, Senior Policy Officer, 20 March
2006.

28   http://www.famyouth.org.uk/pdfs/EveryChildMattersResponse.
pdf

29   NCH, 'Policy and social work research publications',
http://nch.org.uk

30   NFPI Annual Review 2004/2005, p. 5.

31   NFPI Annual Review 2004/2005, p. 4.

32   NFPI Annual Review 2004/2005, p. 13.

33   Commission on Families and the Wellbeing of Children, *Families
and the State: An Inquiry into the Relationship Between the State and the
Family in the Upbringing of Children*, 2005, 'Executive Summary',
p. 5.

34   Commission on Families and the Wellbeing of Children, *Families
and the State*, 2005, 'Executive Summary', p. 10.

35   Charity Commission, CC9: 'Political activities and campaigning by
charities', para. 5, 2004.

36   *Public Action, Private Benefit: A Review of Charities and the Wider Not-
For-Profit Sector*, London: Cabinet Office, 2002, p. 45.

37   Interview with Maurice Wren, director of Asylum Aid, 7 August
2006.

38   Charity Commission, CC9, para. 25.

39   Charity Commission, CC9, para. 23.

40   Charity Commission, CC9, para. 12.

41   Charity Commission, CC9, para. 42.

42   Charity Commission, CC9, para. 13. Emphasis added.

43   'Virtue's intermediaries', *The Economist*, 25 February 2006.

44 'Virtue's intermediaries', *The Economist*, 25 February 2006.

45 Empty Homes Agency Annual Report 2006, pp. 15, 3.

46 Swindon Coalition of Disabled People, Director's report and financial statements for the year ended 31 March 2003.

47 Norfolk Council of Disabled People, Report of the directors and financial statements for the year ended 31 March 2004, p. 7.

48 Standing Conference of Voluntary Organisations for People with a Learning Disability in Wales, Financial statements for the year ended 31 March 2005, p. 9. 'About half from the Welsh Assembly and half from local authorities', as someone in the finance department informed me: telephone conversation, 21 August 2006.

49 Breakthrough UK Limited, Accounts for the year ended 31 March 2005, p. 9.

50 Independent Living Association, Report and financial statements for the year ended 31 March 2004.

51 Community Integrated Care, for example, was established to provide services under contract. It is 99.4 per cent dependent on contracts. See Hanvey and Philpot, *Sweet Charity*, 1996, p. 60.

52 Fathers Direct Annual Report: The tide turns 2004/2005, p. 1.

53 Fathers Direct Annual Report: The tide turns 2004/2005, p. 2.

54 Fathers Direct Annual Report: The tide turns 2004/2005, p. 16. Events funding by government accounts for a potentially huge tranche of the Fathers Direct income. Fathers Direct brags that it hosted 'the biggest ever conference on fatherhood in Europe' (p. 11): it has not been possible to verify whether or not the 'event fees' were derived from the state.

55 http://www.charity-commission.gov.uk/registeredcharities/ search.asp?words=policy+research+bureau&searchby=name&keyT ype=N&limit=200&position=2&OpArea=S&area_of_op=

56 Dartington Hall Trust Report and Accounts for the year ended 31 March 2005.

57 Telephone inquiry, 21 August 2006.

58 See www.prb.org.uk

59 *Public Action, Private Benefit*, 2002, p. 45.

60 'Scope's riding school for disabled facing closure in cash crisis', *Mail on Sunday*, 13 November 2005.

61 http://news.bbc.co.uk/1/hi/wales/1643344.stm

62 Jerrom, C., 'Interview with Martin Narey', *Community Care*, 27 January 2006.

63 Blackmore, *Standing Apart, Working Together*, 2004, p. 28.

64 Neil Churchill, director of communications, Age Concern, quoted in Gibben, Robb and Wilding, *The Third Sector*, 13 March 2002.

65 NSPCC, *Report and Accounts 2006*, NSPCC: London.

66 'Charity reveals campaign spend', *Community Care*, 30 November 2000.

67 *Daily Telegraph*, leader, 25 February 2003.

68 NSPCC, *Report and Accounts 2006*, NSPCC: London.

69 NSPCC, *Report and Accounts 2006*, NSPCC: London.

70 Kirby, T., 'Rag trade tycoon flies 450 guests to charity party in St Petersburg', *Independent*, 26 November 2005.

71 Parkes, T., 'NSPCC must focus on the front line', *Community Care*, 17-23 January, 2002.

72 David Clifford, letter, *Daily Mail*, 14 November 2001.

73 Charity Commission, CC9, para. 46.

74 Womack, S., 'NSPCC told to spend its cash on children, not campaigning', *Daily Telegraph*, 24 February 2003.

75 *Daily Telegraph*, leader, 25 February 2003.

76 http://www.famyouth.org.uk/bulletin.php?number=116

77 Parkes, T., 'NSPCC must focus on the front line', *Community Care*, 17-23 January, 2002.

78 Birkett, D. 'It needs to be stopped. Full stop', *Guardian*, 19 February 2002.

79 'Dangerous game', *Community Care*, 30 November 2000.

80 Birkett, 'It needs to be stopped. Full stop', *Guardian*, 19 February 2002.

81 Heathcoat Amory, E., 'The RSPCA has £16m debts', *Daily Mail*, 22 October 2002.

82 Quoted in Heathcoat Amory, E., 'The RSPCA has £16m debts', *Daily Mail*, 22 October 2002.

83 Harrison, D., 'RSPCA militants want to drop Queen over her support for hunting', *Daily Telegraph*, 13 June 2004.

84 Heathcoat Amory, E., 'The RSPCA has £16m debts', *Daily Mail*, 22 October 2002.

85 *Simmonds v Heffer and others*, [1983] BCLC 298.

86 Heathcoat Amory, E., 'The RSPCA has £16m debts', *Daily Mail*, 22 October 2002.

87 Thompson, A., 'The RSPCA should be saving animals, not hounding MPs', *Daily Telegraph*, 22 October 2002.

88 Charity Commission, CC9, para. 46.

89 Charity Commission, CC9, para. 37.

90 'Concern over new RSPB report', Countryside Alliance press release, 6 March 2006.

91 RSPCA, Trustees' Report and Accounts 2004, p. 12.

92 Charitiy Commission, CC9, para 30.

93 McIntyre, S., 'Why did the RSPCA spend two years and £50,000 prosecuting PC for putting a cat out of its misery?', *Daily Mail*, 10 April 2006.

94 Stanley Brodie, QC, quoted in Copping, J., 'RSPCA investigated over "political" badgers campaign', *Daily Telegraph*, 12 March 2006.

95   Oborne, P., Foreword, in Pye-Smith, C., *Rural Rites: Hunting and the Politics of Prejudice*, London: All Party Parliamentary Middle Way Group, 2006, p. 8.

96   Hobhouse, J., 'Now, an RSPCA insider speaks out,' *Country Illustrated*, Vol. 8, No. 76, December 2005, p. 67.

97   Brown, A., *Who Cares for Animals? 150 Years of the RSPCA*, London: Heinemann, 1974.

98   Including a telephone interview, 11/04/06.

99   Letter from Jackie Ballard to Lord Donoughue, 8 April 2004. Cited in Pye-Smith, C., *Rural Rites*, 2006, p. 74.

100   Pye-Smith, *Rural Rites*, 2006, pp. 47-48.

101   Pye-Smith, *Rural Rites*, 2006, p. 48.

102   Pye-Smith, *Rural Rites*, 2006, p. 51.

103   Quoted in Pye-Smith, *Rural Rites*, 2006, p. 76.

104   Reynolds, J., *Cruelty and Utility: Comments on Principles and Acceptability*, The Game Conservancy Trust: Fordingbridge, 2002, pp. 3-5.

105   Reynolds, *Cruelty and Utility*, 2002, pp. 3-5.

106   Pye-Smith, *Rural Rites*, 2006, p. 78.

107   Pye-Smith, *Rural Rites*, 2006, p. 78.

108   Letter from the Chief Charity Commissioner, 'Animal welfare,' *The Times*, 17 July 1996.

109   Ward, S., 'RSPCA told to put human needs before animal pain', *International News*, April 1996.

110   Ward, S., 'RSPCA told to put human needs before animal pain', *International News*, April 1996.

111   Harrison, D., 'RSPCA militants want to drop Queen over her support for hunting', *Daily Telegraph*, 13 June 2004.

112   Harrison, D., 'RSPCA militants want to drop Queen over her support for hunting', *Daily Telegraph*, 13 June 2004.

113 RSPCA, 'Policies on Animal Welfare', *Declaration of Animal Rights*, 1979.

114 RSPCA, Trustees' Report and Accounts 2004, p. 16.

115 Thompson, A., 'The RSPCA should be saving animals, not hounding MPs', *Daily Telegraph*, 22 October 2002.

116 Pye-Smith, *Rural Rites*, 2006, p. 77.

117 Among these, Lord Willoughby de Broke and Stanley Johnson entered into correspondence with the Charity Commission in 2004 to ask them to investigate whether the political activities of the RSPCA were compatible with their privileged charitable status. They got nowhere.

118 Hobhouse, J., 'Now, an RSPCA insider speaks out,' *Country Illustrated*, vol. 8, no. 76, Christmas 2005, p. 67.

119 'Legal Structure of Amnesty International UK', http://www.amnesty.org.uk/amnesty/aiukstructure.shtml

120 Smith, R. and Whittington, P., *Charity: The Spectre of Over-regulation and State Dependency*, London: CPS, 2006, unpublished draft, p. 51.

5: Bureaucracies of Compassion

1 *UK Voluntary Sector Almanac 2006*, London: NCVO, 2006, pp. 2-3.

2 Pharoah, C., Walker, W., Goodey, L. and Clegg, S., *Charity Trends 2006*, London: CAF, 2006 p. 4.

3 Pharoah, C., Walker, W., Goodey, L. and Clegg, S., *Charity Trends 2005*, London: CAF, 2005, pp. 9, 24.

4 Pharoah, Walker, Goodey and Clegg, *Charity Trends 2006*, 2006, pp. 4, 6. The bottom half of the Top 1,000 only kept pace with inflation.

5 Pharoah, Walker, Goodey and Clegg, *Charity Trends 2006*, p. 6.

6 Pharoah, Walker, Goodey and Clegg, *Charity Trends 2006*, p. 23.

7 Pharoah, Walker, Goodey and Clegg, *Charity Trends 2006*, p. 23.

8 Pharoah, Walker, Goodey and Clegg, *Charity Trends 2006*, p. 23.

9   Pharoah, Walker, Goodey and Clegg, *Charity Trends 2006*, p. 52.

10 The Researching the Voluntary Sector Conference 2004. Report on the 10th annual research conference, Sheffield 2004. Quoted in *UK Voluntary Sector Almanac 2006*, p. 3.

11 Pharoah, Walker, Goodey and Clegg, *Charity Trends 2006*, p. 169.

12 Payne, J., *The Promise of Community*, Indianapolis: Philanthropy Roundtable, 1994, p. 11.

13 Pharoah, Walker, Goodey and Clegg, *Charity Trends 2006*, p. 1.

14 O'Hara, M., 'Prisoner of conscience', *Guardian*, 24 May 2006.

15 Holman, B., letter, *Guardian*, 31 May 2006.

16 Joy, I. and Miller, I., *Don't Mind Me*, London: NPC, 2006, p. 40.

17 Sandford, S. and Lumley, T., *Home Truths*, London: NPC, 2006, p. 53.

18 *The economic and social impact of the women's voluntary and community sector—a pilot study*, London: WRC, 2006, pp. 42-48.

19 Sandford and Lumley, *Home Truths*, 2006, p. 53.

20 *The economic and social impact of the women's voluntary and community sector—a pilot study*, 2006, p. 44.

21 Osborne, S. and Ross, K., 'Regeneration: The Role and Impact of Local Development Agencies', in Harris, M. and Rochester, C. (eds), *Voluntary Organisations and Social Policy in Britain: Perspectives on Change and Choice*, Houndmills: Palgrave, 2001, pp. 81-93.

22 *House of Lords Hansard*, 20 January 2005, Column 938.

23 Griffith, M., Jochum, V. and Wilding, K., *Voluntary Sector Strategic Analysis 2006/07*, London: NCVO, 2006, p. 22. Evidence from the Labour Force Survey indicates that the sector employed 608,000 people in 2004, an increase of 45,000 people since 2000. Cited in *UK Voluntary Sector Almanac 2006*, p. 4.

24 Pharoah, Walker, Goodey and Clegg, *Charity Trends 2006*, pp. 169-173.

25 'Chiefs are not charity cases,' *The Times*, 20 June 2006.

26 Saxton, J., *Charity Times*, May-June 2006. Cited in Smith, R. and
    Whittington, P., *Charity: The Spectre of Over-regulation and State
    Dependency*, London: CPS, 2006, p. 10.

27 Blackmore, A., *Standing Apart, Working Together: A Study of the
    Myths and Realities of Voluntary and Community Sector Independence*,
    London: NCVO, 2004, p. 33.

28 Blake, G., Robinson, D. and Smerdon, M., *Living Values: A Report
    Encouraging Boldness in Third Sector Organisations*, London:
    Community Links, 2006, p. 28.

29 ACEVO is the great champion of this cause—see their website
    http://www.acevo.org.uk/main/index.phpm—for further details,
    but there are others, too, who advocate this line of development.

30 Lewis, J., 'Voluntary Organisations in "New Partnership" with
    Local Authorities: The Anatomy of a Contract', *Social Policy and
    Administration*, 28, (3), 1994.

31 Carpenter, M., *Normality is Hard Work: Trade Unions and the Politics
    of Community Care*, London: Lawrence and Wishart, 1994, p. 80.
    Cited in Hanvey, C. and Philpot, T. (eds), *Sweet Charity: The Role
    and Workings of Voluntary Organisations*, London: Routledge, 1996,
    p. 47.

32 Jones, R., 'Swimming together: The tidal change for statutory
    agencies and the voluntary sector', in Hanvey and Philpot, *Sweet
    Charity*, 1996, p. 47.

33 Griffith, Jochum and Wilding, *Voluntary Sector Strategic Analysis
    2006/07*, 2006, p. 23.

34 Griffith, Jochum and Wilding, *Voluntary Sector Strategic Analysis
    2006/07*, 2006, p. 24.

35 As Kevin Curley, the chief executive of the National Association for
    Voluntary and Community Action, wrote in a letter to the *Guardian*
    in 2006. 'Big is not better', 15 February 2006.

36 Lewis, 'Voluntary Organisations in "New Partnership" with Local
    Authorities', *Social Policy and Administration*, 28, (3), 2004.

37 Pharoah, Walker, Goodey and Clegg, *Charity Trends 2006*, p. 173.

[38] Smith and Whittington, *Charity,* 2006, p. 10. Authors' correspondence with the Charity Commission, 4 January 2006.

[39] Charity Commission, 'Transparency and Accounting', 2004. See also the Charity Commission's RS8, 'Transparency and Accountability, 2006.

[40] Smith and Whittington, *Charity,* 2006, pp. 17-18.

[41] Pharoah, Walker, Goodey and Clegg, *Charity Trends 2006,* p. 29.

[42] NCVO, *UK Voluntary Sector Almanac: The State of the Sector,* http://www.ncvo-vol.org.uk/research/index.asp?id=2380&fID=158

[43] Pharoah, Walker, Goodey and Clegg, *Charity Trends 2006,* p. 4.

[44] Smith and Whittington, *Charity,* 2006, p. 9, using data from the NCVO's *UK Voluntary Sector Almanac 2004.*

[45] Hanvey and Philpot, *Sweet Charity,* 1996, p. 4.

[46] Tanner, M., *The Poverty of Welfare: Helping Others in Civil Society,* Washington: Cato, 2003, p. 105.

[47] Blackmore, *Standing Apart, Working Together,* 2004, p. 34.

[48] *Public Action, Private Benefit: A Review of Charities and the Wider Not-For-Profit Sector,* London: Cabinet Office, 2002, p. 14.

[49] Association of Charitable Foundations Annual Report 2005, p. 24.

[50] Pharoah, Walker, Goodey and Clegg, *Charity Trends 2006,* p. 21.

[51] Bartholomew, J., *The Welfare State We're In,* London: Politico's, 2004, pp. 42-44. He claims that charitable giving in the 'middle classes' has gone down from ten per cent in the 'Victorian Age' to one per cent in 'modern times.' Ann Blackmore (telephone interview 6 June 2006) has disputed those statistics.

[52] Hanvey and Philpot, *Sweet Charity,* 1996,p. 13.

[53] Griffith, Jochum and Wilding, *Voluntary Sector Strategic Analysis 2006/07,* 2006, p. 17.

[54] Pharoah, Walker, Goodey and Clegg, *Charity Trends 2006,* p. 155.

[55] Pharoah, Walker, Goodey and Clegg, *Charity Trends 2006,* p. 4.

[56] Browne-Wilkinson, H., 'Philanthropy in the 21st Century', speech delivered at Institute of Philanthropy / Coutts Conference, 17 June 2004.

[57] Pharoah, Walker, Goodey and Clegg, *Charity Trends 2006*, p. 156.

[58] 2002 Harris Poll, Chronicle of Philanthropy, cited in Hilary Browne-Wilkinson, 'Philanthropy in the 21st Century', speech delivered at Institute of Philanthropy / Coutts Conference, 17 June 2004.

[59] Interview with David Emerson, director of the Association of Charitable Foundations, 6 June 2006.

[60] Browne-Wilkinson, H., 'Philanthropy in the 21st Century', speech delivered at Institute of Philanthropy / Coutts Conference, 17 June 2004.

[61] Andrew Carnegie, *The Gospel of Wealth*, Bedford: Mass., Applewood, 1998, esp. pp. 1, 20-24.

[62] Institute of Philanthropy, 'The Need For Strategic Change In The Voluntary Sector'. http://www.instituteforphilanthropy.org.uk/growth.html

[63] Pharoah, Walker, Goodey and Clegg, *Charity Trends 2006*, p. 165.

[64] Institute of Philanthropy, 'The Need For Strategic Change In The Voluntary Sector'. http://www.instituteforphilanthropy.org.uk/growth.html

[65] Cited by Iain Duncan Smith MP, speech at '*Third Sector* magazine, Britain's Most Admired Charities Awards', 3 November 2005.

[66] Davis Smith, J., 'Volunteers: Making a Difference?', in Harris and Rochester, *Voluntary Organisations and Social Policy in Britain*, 2001, p. 186.

[67] This is how the Home Office Voluntary Services Unit seeks to promote voluntarism. For a good discussion of how voluntarism has been redefined to accommodate the blurred boundaries, see Davis Smith, 'Volunteers: Making a Difference?', in Harris and Rochester, *Voluntary Organisations and Social Policy in Britain*, 2001, pp. 185-198.

68 Quoted in Prochaska, F., *Christianity and Social Service in Modern Britain*, Oxford: Oxford University Press, 2006, p. 158.

69 Blackmore, *Standing Apart, Working Together*, 2004, p. 20.

70 Blake, Robinson and Smerdon, *Living Values*, 2006, pp. 11-12.

71 Himmelfarb, G., *Poverty and Compassion*, New York: Alfred Knopf, 1991, p. 3.

72 Robert Glasgow, 'An Interview with Irving Kristol', *Psychology Today*, February 1974, quoted in Douglas Murray, *Neoconservatism*, p. 74.

6: Nationalising Agencies

1 *Public Action, Private Benefit: A Review of Charities and the Wider Not-For-Profit Sector*, London: Cabinet Office, 2002, p. 19.

2 Though there is currently a hotly contested debate about their status.

3 Les Hems, 'Private Action, Public Benefit: The organisational and institutional landscape of the UK wider nonprofit sector', unpublished submission to the *Public Action, Private Benefit*, 2002.

4 http://www.guidestar.or.uk/gs_summary.aspx?CCReg=209131 &strquery=income(9)

5 Medical Research Council Accounts 2005, p. 41.

6 http://www.guidestar.or.uk/gs_summary.aspx?CCReg=1036733 &strquery=income(9)

7 Richard Brooks and Martin Bailey, 'Gallery fails to profit from man of steel', *Sunday Times*, 11 June 2006.

8 A similar scandal arose in 2005 when the Tate Gallery—which received £30 million a year in subsidy between 2003 and 2005, and almost £9 million from direct donations—paid £700,000 to Chris Ofili, one of its trustees, for a piece of art work. After a nine-month investigation by the Charity Commission, the Tate was found guilty of breaking charity laws in July 2006, and there are ongoing investigations into other such purchases of works by artist-trustees.

The Tate, Tate Report 2002-2004; *Guardian*, 'Emails reveal Ofili's cash deal from Tate', 24 October 2005; *Daily Telegraph*, 'Tate broke charity laws by buying art from its trustees', 19 July 2006.

9   The first National Lottery Act was signed on 21 October 1993. The first draw was held a year later, on 19 November 1994 (www.national-lottery.co.uk/player/p/about/aboutInside. do#anchor01)

10   Lea, R. and Lewis, D., *The Larceny of the Lottery Fund*, London: Centre for Policy Studies, January 2006, p. 5.

11   Conservative Party Manifesto 1992, reproduced in Lea and Lewis, *The Larceny of the Lottery Fund*, 2006, p. ii.

12   Part 1, Section 6 (2), National Lottery Act 1998, http://www.opsi.gov.uk/ACTS/acts1998/80022--b.htm#6

13   Section 7, National Lottery Act 2006, http://www.opsi.gov.uk/acts/acts2006/60023--a.htm#7

14   Lea and Lewis, *The Larceny of the Lottery Fund*, 2006, p. i.

15   National Lottery website, http://www.national-lottery.co.uk/player/information.do?info=wheremoneygoes

16   Lea and Lewis, *The Larceny of the Lottery Fund*, 2006, p. 12.

17   Lea and Lewis, *The Larceny of the Lottery Fund*, 2006, p. 2.

18   Linklater, M., *The Times*, 2 June 2004.

19   Stokes, P., 'Lottery rejects Samaritans', *Daily Telegraph*, 10 February 2005.

20   Pharoah, C., Walker, W., Goodey, L. and Clegg, S., *Charity Trends 2006*, London: CAF, 2006, p. 5.

21   Griffith, M., Jochum, V. and Wilding, K., *Voluntary Sector Strategic Analysis 2006/07*, London: NCVO, 2006, p. 27. The ACF is also concerned about this: see *ACF Annual Report 2005*, London: ACF, 2006, p. 24.

22   Source: http://212.58.240.36/2/low/uk_news/england/london/4669420.stm

[23] Tessa Jowell's keynote address to the 10th annual Lottery Monitor conference at the British Museum, 21 June 2006. http://www.culture.gov.uk/global/press_notices/archive_2006/ jowell_lottery_monitor_speech.htm)

[24] Blackmore, A., *Standing Apart, Working Together: A Study of the Myths and Realities of Voluntary and Community Sector Independence,* London: NCVO, 2004, p. 9.

[25] Charity Commission, RR7: 'The Independence of Charities from the State', section 2, 2001.

[26] RR7, section 6.

[27] RR7, section 7.

[28] Smith, R. and Whittington, P., *Charity: The Spectre of Over-regulation and State Dependency,* London: CPS, 2006, unpublished draft, p. 20, citing research by the Charity Commission.

[29] Chapman, R., 'Are charities the new public sector', *Guardian,* 21 March 2006.

[30] Smith and Whittington, *Charity,* 2006, unpublished draft, p. 20, citing the Annual Review of Charity at the Charity Commission.

[31] Smith and Whittington, *Charity,* 2006, unpublished draft, p. 20, citing a private telephone conversation.

[32] *UK Voluntary Sector Almanac 2006,* London: NCVO, 2006.

[33] *UK Voluntary Sector Almanac 2006,*

[34] RR7, section 5.

[35] Charity Commission, 'Public Service Delivery by Charities – Commission Decision in (i) Trafford Community Leisure Trust ("TCLT") and (ii) Wigan Leisure and Culture Trust ("WLCT"), *passim.*

[36] Charity Commission, 'Policy Statement on Charities and Public Service Delivery', p. 1. Also: Charity Commission, 'Public Service Delivery by Charities – Commission Decision in (i) Trafford Community Leisure Trust ("TCLT") and (ii) Wigan Leisure and Culture Trust ("WLCT"), p. 2.

37 Charity Commission, 'Public Service Delivery by Charities –
    Commission Decision in (i) Trafford Community Leisure Trust
    ("TCLT") and (ii) Wigan Leisure and Culture Trust ("WLCT"), p. 9.

38 Wigan Leisure & Culture Trust, Annual Review and Report,
    2004/2005, p. 21. A number of telephone calls were inconclusive
    and no messages were returned.

39 Charity Commission, 'Public Service Delivery by Charities –
    Commission Decision in (i) Trafford Community Leisure Trust
    ("TCLT") and (ii) Wigan Leisure and Culture Trust ("WLCT"), p. 7.

40 Some might argue that they already have been: see Prochaska, F.,
    Philanthropy and the Hospitals of London: the Kings Fund 1897-1990,
    Oxford: Clarendon Press, 1992, pp. 228-29.

41 Charity Commission, 'Public Service Delivery by Charities –
    Commission Decision in (i) Trafford Community Leisure Trust
    ("TCLT") and (ii) Wigan Leisure and Culture Trust ("WLCT"), p. 6.

42 Malpass, P., 'The Restructuring of Social Rented Housing in
    Britain: Demunicipalization and the Rise of "Registered Social
    Landlords"', *European Journal of Housing Policy*, vol. 1, no. 1, 2001, 3.

43 Mocroft, I., and Zimmeck, M., *Central Government Funding of
    Voluntary and Community Organisations 1982/83 to 2001/02*, London:
    Home Office, 2004, p. 5, 18.

44 Mocroft and Zimmeck, *Central Government Funding of Voluntary and
    Community Organisations 1982/83 to 2001/02*, 2004, p. 4.

45 Malpass, P., and Mullins, D., 'Local Authority Housing Stock
    Transfer in the UK: From Local Initiative to National Policy',
    Housing Studies, vol. 17, no. 4, 2002, 675.

46 Mullins, D., and Riseborough, M., 'Non-profit Housing Agencies',
    in Harris, M. and Rochester, C. (eds), *Voluntary Organisations and
    Social Policy in Britain: Perspectives on Change and Choice*,
    Houndmills: Palgrave, 2001, p. 156.

47 Malpass, P., 'Housing Associations and Housing Policy in Britain
    Since 1989, *Housing Studies*, vol. 14, no. 6, 1999, 891.

48 Malpass, 'The Restructuring of Social Rented Housing in Britain: Demunicipalization and the Rise of "Registered Social Landlords"', *European Journal of Housing Policy*, vol. 1, no. 1, 2001, 4.

49 *House Styles: Performance and Pricing in Housing Management*, London: Audit Commission, 1996, p. 10.

50 Charity Commission, 'Guidance for Charitable Registered Social Landlords', 2004.

51 www.england.shelter.org.uk/policy/policy-936.cfm. Emphasis added.

52 Blackmore, *Standing Apart, Working together*, 2004, p. 19.

53 Joseph Rowntree Foundation, *Findings: Housing Research 202*, February 1997, summarising *Contemporary Patterns of Residential Mobility in Relation of Social Housing in England*, York: Centre for Housing Policy.

54 Parker, F., *George Peabody: A Biography*, Nashville: Vanderbilt Press, 1995, p. 150.

55 Parker, *George Peabody*, 1995, p. 128.

56 *Peabody Trust Inspection Report*, London: Audit Commission, 2004, p. 5.

57 *Peabody Trust Inspection Report*, 2004, pp. 49-50.

58 Manzi, T. and Smith Bowers, B., 'So Many Managers, So Little Vision: Registered Social Landlords and Consortium Schemes in the UK', *European Journal of Housing Policy*, vol. 4, no. 1, April 2004, 72.

59 Ginsburg, N., 'The Privatisation of Council Housing', *Critical Social Policy*, vol. 25, no. 1, 126-127.

60 Manzi and Smith Bowers, 'So Many Managers, So Little Vision: Registered Social Landlords and Consortium Schemes in the UK', *European Journal of Housing Policy*, Vol. 4, No. 1, April 2004, 73.

61 http://society.guardian.co.uk/salarysurvey/table/0,,1034758,00.html

62 Malpass, P., 'Housing Associations and Housing Policy in Britain Since 1989', *Housing Studies*, vol. 14, no. 6, 1999, 892.

7: Where Do We Go From Here?

1   *Public Action, Private Benefit: A Review of Charities and the Wider Not-For-Profit Sector*, London: Cabinet Office, 2002, p. 62.

2   *Public Action, Private Benefit*, p. 79.

3   *Public Action, Private Benefit*, p. 85.

4   *Public Action, Private Benefit*, p. 86.

5   NCVO press release, 'Charities club together to improve public understanding of the voluntary sector', 11 July 2005.

6   Benjamin, A., 'Charities at risk as donations from public lag behind state funding', *Guardian*, 10 August 2006.

7   Toynbee, P., 'Compassionate Conservatism sounds uncannily familiar', *Guardian*, 13 June 2006.

8   Pharoah, C., Walker, W., Goodey, L. and Clegg, S., *Charity Trends 2005*, London: CAF, 2005, p. 4.

9   *Public Action, Private Benefit*, p. 69.

10   *Public Action, Private Benefit*, p. 70.

11   Blackmore, A., *Standing Together, Working apart: A Study of the Myths and Realities of Voluntary and Community Sector Independence*, London: NCVO, 2004, p. 36.

12   *Giving Confidently: The Role of the Charity Commission in Regulating Charities*, London: National Audit Office, 25 October 2001, p. 1.

13   'Regulation by the Charity Commission', *First Report of the Joint Committee on the Draft Charities Bill*, http://www.parliament.the-stationery-office.co.uk/pa/jt200304/jtselect/jtchar/167/16706.htm

14   *Giving Confidently*, National Audit Office, 2001, p. 1.

15   *Giving Confidently*, National Audit Office, 2001, p. 3.

16   *Public Action, Private Benefit*, p. 80.

17   *Public Action, Private Benefit*, p. 71.

18   *Public Action, Private Benefit*, p. 80.

[19] Pharoah, Walker, Goodey and Clegg, *Charity Trends 2006*, pp. 101-102. In fact, the total income and expenditure of the UK's 9,000 trusts and foundations is not known. See Siederer, N., 'Giving in trust: The role of the grant-making trust', in Hanvey, C. and Philpot, T. (eds), *Sweet Charity: The Role and Workings of Voluntary Organisations*, London: Routledge, 1996, p. 116; and ACF *Annual Report 2005*, p. 20. The words 'trust' and 'foundation' are virtually synonymous. All charitable foundations are trusts—that is, they're managed by trustees, who may or may not be supported by paid staff. A foundation is a trust whose income derives from an endowment of land or invested capital. Not all foundations make grants; some use their income to finance charitable work of their own. Not all grant-making trusts have an endowment. (Trust refers here to grant-making charities of any sort.)

[20] Leat, D., 'Grant-Making Foundations: Policy Shapers or Policy Takers?', in Harris, M. and Rochester, C. (eds), *Voluntary Organisations and Social Policy in Britain: Perspectives on Change and Choice*, Houndmills: Palgrave, 2001, p. 125.

[21] Interviews with Peter Kilgarrif director Lankelly-Chase Foundation, 6 July 2006; and David Emerson, director Association of Charitable Foundations, 7 July 2006.

[22] Interview with Cathy Pharoah, 3 June 2006.

[23] A good overview is provided by Siederer, 'Giving in trust: The role of the grant-making trust', in Hanvey and Philpot, *Sweet Charity*, 1996, pp. 111-127.

[24] The Baring Foundation Report on Activities, London, 2005, p. 8.

[25] *ACF Annual Report 2005*, p. 20.

[26] *ACF Annual Report 2005*, p. 24.

[27] *ACF Annual Report 2005*, p. 24.

[28] Chapman, R., 'Are charities the new public sector?', *Guardian*, 21 March 2006.

[29] See Blackmore, A., Bush, H. and Bhutta, M., *The Reform of Public Services: The Role of the Voluntary Sector*, London: NCVO, Annex A, 2005.

[30] Haldane, D., 'The Lottery and the arts', *Trust and Foundation News*, June/July 1997, p. 17, cited in Leat, 'Grant-Making Foundations: Policy Shapers or Policy Takers?', in Harris and Rochester, *Voluntary Organisations and Social Policy in Britain*, 2001, p. 131.

[31] Quoted in Smith, R., and Whittington, P., *Charity: The Spectre of Over-regulation and State Dependency*, London: CPS, 2006, p. 27.

[32] Written evidence to the Joint Committee on the Draft Bill, 'Supplementary memorandum from the Association of Charitable Foundations (DCH 276)', Annex 2. Cited in CPS *Charity*, p. 28. A good discussion of the issues can also be found in Leat, D., 'Grant-Making Foundations: Policy Shapers or Policy Takers?' in Harris and Rochester, p. 133.

[33] 'Virtue's intermediaries', *The Economist*, 25 February 2006.

[34] See for instance: Harker, A. and Burkeman, S., *Stepping up the Stairs: Increasing the Impact of Progressive Philanthropy in the UK*, London: Carnegie UK Trust, 2005.

[35] http://www.communityfoundations.org.uk/about_community _foundations/frequently_asked_questions.php

[36] Pharoah, Walker, Goodey and Clegg, *Charity Trends 2006*, 113.

[37] Tocqueville, A. de, *Democracy in America*, Modern Library edn., New York, 1981, pp. 556, 578.

[38] 'Public service delivery: are charities leaping to their deaths?' Directory of Social Change. http://www.dsc.org.uk/aboutdsc/enews/enews-issue39.html

[39] 'Senior Labour figures set out a new vision for public service reform, following compelling research', 6 May 2004. http://www.acevo.org.uk/main/index.php?content=newsitem&new s_id=47

Index